ASHES TO FLAMES

ASHES TO FLAMES

A Lenten Pilgrimage

Ronald D. Witherup, PSS

Paulist Press
New York / Mahwah, NJ

Cover image by Shutterstock.com
Cover design by Sharyn Banks
Book design by Lynn Else

Library of Congress Control Number: 2024943778

ISBN 978-0-8091-5753-2 (paperback)
ISBN 978-0-8091-8920-5 (ebook)

Published by Paulist Press
997 Macarthur Boulevard
Mahwah, NJ 07430
www.paulistpress.com

Printed and bound in the
United States of America

CONTENTS

ACKNOWLEDGMENTS

Thanks to my friend and colleague Fr. Thomas R. Hurst, PSS, for some helpful suggestions while reading an earlier draft of this book, and to Paul McMahon for the invitation to write it.

INTRODUCTION
A Few Words about Lent

Lent evokes three kinds of responses. One embraces it as a time to set one's spiritual life in order; another dreads it as a long and arduous road to Easter requiring many sacrifices. A third simply ignores it or sees it as an irrelevant Christian invention hardly worthy of attention in today's bustling world.

Lent is countercultural. It can be seen as disruptive, a distraction from ordinary life. For believing Christians of almost every denomination, Lent cannot be ignored. It is an essential season of the liturgical year, a time of renewal and, in the Northern Hemisphere, a harbinger of spring. In fact, the word "Lent" comes from Middle English *lente*, meaning *spring*. It is meant to be a season of spiritual rebirth, a time to prepare us to celebrate the paschal feast of Easter. To borrow an expression from the world of computers, Lent is an opportunity to "reboot." If we are honest, we acknowledge that our spiritual and moral lives have sometimes been tarnished. We are stained by sin, selfishness, and a disordered life. But Lent says we don't have to stay that way. There is a chance for new beginnings.

This book offers a guide to this rich liturgical season as a kind of armchair pilgrimage. Although readers need to take a metaphorical "step" to begin this pilgrimage throughout the seven weeks of the season, you need not actually step outside. Instead, I invite you to take ten to fifteen minutes a day to meditate on the riches that this season offers.

A WORD ABOUT HISTORY

To begin, I want to place Lent in its proper context, historically and spiritually. Virtually all Christians recognize Lent as a period of forty days of penance, fasting, and spiritual exercises leading up to Easter. But how did it come about?

The contemporary forty-day period did not appear until the fourth century, at the time of the Council of Nicaea (325 CE), so seventeen hundred years ago. It likely began as an observance for catechumens, those preparing for baptism and entrance into the church at Easter. The number forty is symbolic and stems from the biblical use of this number for a significantly long period of time. It is not necessarily meant to be taken literally, yet the images from the biblical data are impressive. Consider the following incomplete list:

- When God threatens to destroy the earth God created, the method is by rain for forty days and forty nights (Gen 7:4, 12).
- The Israelites wandered in the desert and ate manna there for forty years (Exod 16:35; Deut 2:7).
- Moses went up the mountain to encounter God and stayed there forty days and forty nights (Exod 24:18; 34:28; Deut 9:9).
- The prophet Elijah spent forty days and forty nights on his journey to Mount Horeb, God's mountain, while fleeing his enemies (1 Kgs 19:8).
- Jesus spent forty days and forty nights in the wilderness (like the Israelites before him) being tempted prior to beginning his public ministry (Matt 4:2; also Mark 1:13 and Luke 4:2).
- Jesus appears to his disciples over a forty-day period after his resurrection (Acts 1:3).

Not all of these examples were of equal value in the design of Lent. Most likely, the images of Moses, Elijah, and Jesus were the inspiration for a forty-day spiritual journey. The point, however, is not to get hung up on the numbers but to recognize a sufficiently long period of time for God's grace to accomplish something special. In fact, the numbering of the days of Lent is not as simple as it might seem.

As Lent developed, it began as six weeks of six days, with Sundays being excluded from the count because Sunday is the day of the Resurrection, not a penitential day. That yielded only thirty-six days. But to conform to the biblical ideal of forty days of fasting, the Roman church in the seventh century added four days prior to the First Sunday of Lent, from Ash Wednesday to the following Saturday. This supplied four more days, which now rounds out our current forty-day Lenten experience.

In this book, I emphasize this forty-day period as a spiritual pilgrimage. It begins with ashes—the ashes we receive on our foreheads on Ash Wednesday, which inaugurate the season—and concludes with the flames at the Easter Vigil on Holy Saturday night. This may seem paradoxical. Normally, ashes are the result of fire. During Lent, this is reversed. The ashes remind us that we were created from the dust of the earth (Gen 2:7). Ultimately, that is our fleshly destiny. With the new fire, from which our Easter candles are lit, the light casts out the darkness. From the ashes, new life arises. What begins in dark ashes springs to brilliance in the flames of Easter. That Lent is a pilgrimage should also be evident. As Moses led Israel through the desert to the promised land and as Jesus fasted for forty days and nights before beginning his mission, which would culminate in Jerusalem, so we take our own spiritual journeys during this sacred time.

Nowadays, many obstacles inhibit our free entrance into this transformative season. Here are a few examples:

- the hectic pace of modern life, with its job obligations and family responsibilities;
- expanding social commitments and the increasing influence of social media, which take up time;

- the noisiness around us—at work, at home, in stores, in public spaces—and the minimal appreciation of the value of silence;
- a decreased acceptance of delayed gratification, and resistance to making lasting commitments.

Overcoming such obstacles remains a challenge for contemporary believers, but the struggle is worth it spiritually.

Readers should also recall that in some years certain major feasts interrupt the normal flow of the liturgical season. Examples include the solemnity of St. Joseph and the solemnity of the Annunciation. In this book, we will bypass such celebrations in favor of maintaining the integrity of the Lenten pilgrimage.

Note also that Lent technically ends at midnight on the Wednesday of Holy Week. Why? Because Holy Thursday, Good Friday, and Holy Saturday are a separate reality, the Triduum, the three holiest days of the liturgical year. They are outside the Lenten season and prepare for the solemnity of Easter. Their focus is unique and centered on the passion, death, and resurrection of Jesus. In this, they are less penitential in character and more oriented to meditating on the salvation achieved by Jesus's voluntary death on a cross.

THE RHYTHM AND FLOW OF LENT

In present Catholic practice, Lent follows the cycle outlined in the lectionary, the approved book of readings, for the liturgy for each year. There are three liturgical years: A (Gospel of Matthew), B (Gospel of Mark), and C (Gospel of Luke). The Gospel of John is used throughout the Lenten and Easter seasons, and John's version of the passion of Jesus is always read on Good Friday. The Sundays utilize the three distinct Synoptic Gospels and thus provide a unique orientation each year. It is instructive to see how Lent unfolds in the design of the lectionary.

Introduction

Lent kicks off the season with the dramatic call to repentance, symbolized by the imposition of ashes on our foreheads in the shape of a cross. The following three days join Ash Wednesday to focus our attention on penitential practices and attitudes that should be characteristic of our Lenten engagement. The First Sunday of Lent always portrays the temptation of Jesus in the wilderness, while the Second Sunday always celebrates the Transfiguration accounts in the Synoptics. Thus, in these first weeks we see Jesus as the model for how to resist temptation by the devil, and we also get a glimpse of his coming glory, since we know he will be victorious over sin and death. Throughout the first three full weeks of Lent, the focus in many of the readings is on our duty to repent and believe in the gospel. We are reminded to reform our lives and live according to God's law. The ancient practices of prayer, fasting, and almsgiving are particularly pertinent throughout Lent.

Then in the fourth week of Lent, a shift takes place. No longer are we the focus. Jesus comes to the fore, especially in his relationship to his heavenly Father. We are invited to meditate on him and on how he was utterly devoted to doing the will of his Father. The fifth week shifts yet again. While the focus remains on Jesus, the readings recount increased opposition to him and his teaching. The intensity builds as Jesus's enemies try to trap him and do away with him. Many readings come from John 8, the great opposition chapter. Finally, in the last week of Lent, which is launched with Palm Sunday, we see where the hostility to Jesus leads. He is ultimately betrayed, denied, and deserted by his own disciples. Yet he surrenders to his enemies in fulfillment of both the ancient Scriptures and his heavenly Father's plan for salvation. Ultimately, this week culminates in the three holy days called the Triduum: Holy Thursday, Good Friday, and Holy Saturday. Lent reaches its climax in the paradox of the cross and the hope of the resurrection.

The following two charts might help to visualize how Lent thus plays out.

TABLE 1. SUNDAY READINGS IN LENT

Sundays	Year A (Matthew)	Year B (Mark)	Year C (Luke)
I.	Temptation of Jesus	Temptation of Jesus	Temptation of Jesus
II.	Transfiguration	Transfiguration	Transfiguration
III.	Samaritan woman	Temple incident	Repentance
IV.	Man born blind	Nicodemus	Prodigal father
V.	Lazarus	The Hour arrives	Adulterous woman
Palm Sunday	Entrance into Jerusalem	Entrance into Jerusalem	Entrance into Jerusalem
The Passion	Passion according to Matthew	Passion according to Mark	Passion according to Luke

TABLE 2. WEEKDAY READINGS IN LENT

Weekdays	Ash Wednesday to First Saturday	Weeks 1–3	Weeks 4–5	Holy Week
Focus	Call to repentance and conversion	Exhortation to practices and attitudes	Jesus and his relationship to God the Father	Jesus in his passion and death
Themes	Repent and believe in the gospel	Need for a righteous lifestyle and forgiveness of sins	Increased opposition to Jesus by enemies	Jesus as the Suffering Servant; dramatic passion narrative of John's Gospel
				Triduum

A WORD ABOUT SCRIPTURE

This book follows the flow of the liturgical season as in the revised lectionary, used by Roman Catholics and other denominations. Our reflections will revolve primarily around the Scripture readings that are offered every day of Lent. On weekdays, that means a first reading, a psalm response, and a gospel reading. On Sundays, it means a first reading, a psalm response, a second reading, and a gospel reading. Many times, these readings coalesce nicely into a thematic unity. Sometimes, however, the readings have their own individual messages. The first reading often recounts aspects of salvation history evident in the Old Testament, while the second reading expounds various aspects of Christian identity in baptism. The gospel speaks of incidents from Jesus's earthly ministry with foreshadowing of his future suffering. I have taken this diversity seriously and, since my reflections are only intended as one way of looking at the readings, much is left to the reader to pick and choose what seems most helpful.

Why are the Scriptures so prominent in the Lenten season? First and foremost, because we believe them to be God's divinely inspired word. These ancient texts, ever new in their interpretation and application, are nothing less than a living word among us. St. Paul said it best, when he wrote to the Romans: "For whatever was written previously was written for our instruction, that by endurance and by the encouragement of the scriptures we might have hope" (Rom 15:4). The Scriptures, then, are for *our* use. They can teach us, encourage us, sustain us, and undergird our hope, despite what sometimes can seem hopeless.

At times, readers will note that my chosen theme of the day comes from the Old Testament. This is most appropriate and should not be overlooked because the Old Testament was *the* Sacred Scriptures for Jesus, Peter, Paul, and the early Christians. It took many decades for the New Testament writings to achieve the status of canonical sacred writings. Now, of course, from our Christian perspective, we see the unity of both Testaments. *Dei Verbum*, the Second Vatican Council's Dogmatic Constitution on Divine Revelation (1965), explains this relationship thus:

> God, the inspirer and author of the books of both Testaments, in his wisdom has so brought it about that the New should be hidden in the Old and that the Old should be made manifest in the New. (*Dei Verbum* 16)

We thus need to remain open to the divine message embedded in both Testaments.

Astute readers will notice that I include the psalms in the readings of the day. While I only reference the psalm number, and not the individual verses that are excerpted in the lectionary for the responsorial, nevertheless the psalms can be read with profit. They are easily overlooked in favor of either the first reading or the gospel reading. In my experience, however, the psalms are an important resource for prayer. They can provide the very words we seek to express our personal prayers to God. Two of these psalms come up more than once, Psalm 51 (known as the *Miserere*) and Psalm 130 (known as the *De Profundis*) because of their intense cries for mercy and appeals for repentance. Psalm 22 and Psalm 69 also figure prominently because of their connection to the passion of Jesus Christ. Such psalms as these four find a proper home especially in the Lenten season.

All the psalms taken together, in fact, are unique Sacred Scripture. They are the only place in the Bible where they represent more our word to God rather than God's word to us, though they are both. Once in a while, then, I choose a phrase from the psalm of the day for the theme. I encourage you not to overlook these beautiful, poetic prayers, which speak to us today as directly as they did when they were first composed.

A WORD ABOUT CONTEXT

Year after year, Lent plays out in roughly the same way. It is a permanent liturgical season with its own rhythms and emphases. However, from time to time, other special contexts arise that might influence the way in which we would celebrate Lent. For example, the year 2025 was also a Holy (or Jubilee) Year, the first since the year 2000 at the beginning of the third Christian millennium. Pope Francis proclaimed 2025 a pilgrimage year with the theme of "hope." He also invited special prayers for the environment throughout Lent, based on his teachings on a proper Christian response to climate change, as expressed in the encyclical letter *Laudato Si'* (2015) and his urgent apostolic exhortation *Laudate Deum* (2023). Such unique thematic emphases, whether on the level of the universal church or of the local diocese, may impact the way Lent should be celebrated in a new context. Readers are invited to take such unique circumstances into account in their Lenten meditations.

A WORD ABOUT CHRISTIAN INITIATION

By ancient tradition, Lent is also a customary time for the rites of Christian initiation. After the Second Vatican Council, the Roman Catholic Church restored this ancient practice of preparing catechumens and candidates for baptism or full communion in the Catholic Church. Now called the Order of Christian Initiation of Adults (OCIA), the main ceremonies take place on the Third, Fourth, and Fifth Sundays of Lent, leading up to the baptismal rite at the Easter Vigil. The biblical readings for the Sundays of Liturgical Year A are specifically designed for this process. They are accompanied by a ceremony called the "scrutinies" in which those seeking to be baptized or fully united with the church publicly make clear their desire to join the community of faith. These occasions also provide an opportunity for the congregation to pray earnestly for these seekers.

The reflections offered for these three Sundays of Lent in Year A may be used in any year. They have long and dramatic readings from John's Gospel that are particularly pertinent to welcoming people to the Christian faith. They involve Jesus's encounters with three separate individuals: the Samaritan woman at the well (John 4:4–

42); the man born blind (John 9:1–41); and Lazarus, whom Jesus raises from the dead (John 11:1–45). Thematically, these readings concern water, light, and life, the three main themes that converge at the Easter Vigil. In the event your parish is using these readings for those days, my reflections are geared to their special themes.

HOW TO USE THIS BOOK

This book is intended as a starting point for personal reflections and meditation. For convenience, the Scripture readings of each day of Lent are listed. Ideally, readers can peruse these texts in their own Bible and choose from them insights that seem most pertinent. I have taken the liberty, however, to choose a theme for each day that emerges from the readings. That theme, along with the readings themselves, orient a short reflection.

To make the most of this book, I suggest a brief three-step process:

1. After inviting God to send you the Holy Spirit to open your mind, your heart, and your soul to the sacred word for each day, read the Scriptures of the day, or at least reflect on the chosen excerpt.
2. Read the reflection and spend a couple of minutes in quiet meditation.
3. Conclude with a brief prayer of thanksgiving to God for the gift of this word during Lent.

Many readers might be familiar with an ancient practice of reflecting on the Scriptures called *lectio divina*, which means "prayerful reading." Practiced regularly in monasteries according to various models and promoted by the late Pope Benedict XVI, *lectio* (as it is called) basically means sitting and reflecting on the Scriptures in an unhurried manner. If your time allows, I encourage you to employ this useful method of *praying* the Scriptures (not simply *reading* them). The process need not take long. The key is to open yourself to the Holy Spirit's prompting when you read a passage, perhaps a little slower than normal. Focus on a word, a phrase, or a key image that somehow speaks to you. Sit with it for a few minutes. Then thank God for whatever insight you may have gained and go on with your day.

1

THE FIRST FOUR DAYS

ASH WEDNESDAY

THEME: No Going Back?

READINGS: Joel 2:12–18; Ps 51; 2 Cor 5:20—6:2; Matt 6:1–6, 16–18

"Return to me with your whole heart, with fasting, with weeping, and mourning" (Joel 2:12).

REFLECTION: Once while driving on a vacation in a foreign country, I came to a very small hillside village and was trying to maneuver the rental car up a steep, windy, narrow street to my destination. As the road kept closing in on me, my passengers and I began to get increasingly nervous (this was pre-GPS days). One called out, "You'd better go back; it's getting too narrow; we'll never get through." But there was no way to turn around, and backing up would have been difficult, indeed, impossible: there were two cars behind me! We did finally get through, for the road was able to accommodate small European cars. But I never quite shook off the feeling that, when there is no going back, you never know what will happen.

What if life were like that? What if there was never a chance to say, "I'm sorry" or "Please forgive me"? What if we were always stuck heading in the same direction no matter what we said or did or did not do, and then suddenly came to the recognition that we were in a pickle.

Sadly, some people think God operates this way, but Lent proclaims otherwise. Lent speaks loudly and clearly that there is a path back. No need to keep on going straight ahead to our own possible doom. Each of us has actions or words we regretted. Each of us has circumstances when, to our personal embarrassment, we may not have acted in the most forthright, honest, or righteous way. If that were all there was to human existence, we would be in a sorry state. Fortunately for us, Lent offers an extended time of reflection when we can consider the path we are on. The prophet Joel cries out God's invitation fervently: "Return to me with your whole heart, with fasting, with weeping, and mourning." That is why we mark our foreheads with ashes and the sign of the cross. We signal our willingness to go back, to return to the ways of God, and to abandon the thoughts of mere mortals (see Matt 16:23).

Lent is the season of repentance. Historically, it centered on three biblical actions—prayer, fasting, and almsgiving. It includes additional activities such as other spiritual devotions, abstaining from meat on certain days, perhaps avoiding favorite treats like dessert, wine, alcohol, or movies. But most importantly, it means turning our lives around—conversion (Greek *metanoia*) and getting on the right path.

Even if you think you are in a spiritual cul-de-sac, there is a way out. Heed the call of the prophet! Heed the call of Jesus! We do not do such activities to draw attention to ourselves, but to sincerely try to get our life in order. The good news is that if we admit our failings and our sinfulness, the path back to the Lord is wide open for our return. It leads to a loving and forgiving God who never ceases to call us.

QUESTION: How ready am I to take up the invitation to "repent and believe the good news," the words with which ashes are placed on our foreheads?

THURSDAY AFTER ASH WEDNESDAY

THEME: The Two Paths

READINGS: Deut 30:15–20; Ps 1; Luke 9:22–25

"I have set before you life and prosperity, death and doom....Choose life" (Deut 30:15).

REFLECTION: Isn't the choice evoked in today's Old Testament readings really a "no-brainer"? Who wouldn't choose life over death, prosperity over doom? And yet people do. Motives are often complex, but other values interfere with the choice. If we think we can "get away with it," we may try something that we intuitively know is wrong, illegal, or immoral. Spiritual death ensues.

I once heard a joke about an airline passenger on a long flight. When the flight attendant arrived and asked if he would be eating lunch, the passenger asked, "What are the choices?" The immediate response, delivered with a scowl, was, "Yes or no!"

The Bible has multiple examples of the stark choice between one path or another, life or death, salvation or damnation. The psalm response today is the very first psalm, part of the wisdom tradition. It illustrates the stark choice Moses set before the Israelites in the desert, recounted in the first reading, with a beautiful contrast. The righteous are "like a tree / planted near streams of water" that will flourish. "But not so are the wicked, not so! / They are like chaff driven by the wind." There are but two paths. One is righteous, the other unrighteous. One leads to prosperity, the other to destruction.

We know, of course, that life does not always work out that way. When bad things happen to good people—people who made the right choice—we might ask: Why bother? Neither the psalmist nor Moses naively promises literal blessings in every aspect of human existence when we follow God's law. Jesus, too, gets into the act in today's gospel reading. He urges his followers to pick up their cross

15

"daily" and follow him. Losing your life paradoxically means saving it in the world to come. Yet the choice must be made. The path may be long, rocky, and strewn with obstacles, but sometimes the more difficult route is precisely the one that leads to the greater result. On this second day of Lent, we are reminded of the choice that must be made.

QUESTION: Am I willing to make sacrifices to choose to do what is right before God and humanity, not for reward, but just because it is the right thing to do?

FRIDAY AFTER ASH WEDNESDAY

THEME: A Heart Contrite and Humbled

READINGS: Isa 58:1–9a; Ps 51; Matt 9:14–15

"A heart contrite and humbled, O God, / you will not spurn" (Ps 51:19).

REFLECTION: Something sinister sometimes lingers in the human heart. Think, for instance, of the kind of joy people take when someone generally held in high esteem is caught in an outrageous scandal. While we love to see people succeed, when they "over-succeed" or become arrogantly boastful of their achievements, how we love to see them fall! The Germans have a word for it— *Schadenfreude*—a kind of mischievous glee at someone's downfall, someone who needed to be knocked down a peg or two. It has happened to political leaders, actors and entertainers, star athletes, corporation heads, church leaders, and so on. It also happened in the Bible. The biggest example is King David.

I highlight Psalm 51 today because it is *the* stellar example of a penitential psalm. It will reappear several times throughout Lent. Its heading in the Bible attributes its creation to none other than King David, the greatly exalted ruler of Israel and reputed musician creator of the psalms. The psalmist explains that David composed it after being confronted by the prophet Nathan for his outrageous adultery with Bathsheba (verse 2) and subsequent murder of her husband (see the whole bloody tale in 2 Sam 11—12). How crude can you be? The bigger the person, the harder they fall.

But the psalm reveals a different outcome, not glee but heartfelt remorse and repentance. The psalm testifies to a man who looked deeply into his soul, saw his spectacular failures, and humbly asked God for forgiveness. That is why David remains a great hero, indeed, establishing the line that led to the Messiah, whom we proclaim to be Jesus of Nazareth. But to reach this point of repentance, we have to recognize our own failures, our sins, our hidden weaknesses. God does not condemn a truly contrite heart! Psalm 51 is so important in our Judeo-Christian tradition that it is prayed every Friday morning in the Liturgy of the Hours by the ordained and religious.

QUESTION: Am I able honestly to confront my sinfulness and trust in God's mercy?

SATURDAY AFTER
ASH WEDNESDAY

THEME: The Call

READINGS: Isa 58:9b–14; Ps 86; Luke 5:27–32

"Those who are healthy do not need a physician. I have not come to call the righteous to repentance but sinners" (Luke 5:32).

REFLECTION: Pope Francis has remarked on numerous occasions that his personal motto *miserando atque eligendo*—Latin for "by God's merciful choice"—comes from the description of the call of St. Matthew in Matthew's Gospel (called Levi in Luke 5:27) in the Vulgate (common Latin) edition of the Bible. It is famously illustrated in a painting by Caravaggio that tourists flock to see in the church of San Luigi dei Francesi (St. Louis of France) in Rome. Today's gospel reading is the Lukan version of this famous call of one of the Twelve, the tax collector whom we know as Matthew.

Striking in this call scene is the simple exchange between Jesus and Levi. Jesus says simply, "Follow me." The response is immediate and without question: "And leaving everything behind, he got up and followed him." No questions asked, no hesitation, no plea for some time to think about it. No, he leaves everything and follows! That is the nature of the divine call and of Jesus's call to discipleship. There is no time for discussion or for bargaining. You are either in or out. You either accept or you don't.

Most importantly, however, is to see in the pope's motto an ulterior explanation of this remarkable call. God's merciful outreach to a tax collector—someone despised by the general Jewish population of the day as unscrupulous and cooperating with the enemy Romans—orients this dramatic scene. God's mercy has already touched Matthew, even though he did not recognize it. In Caravaggio's painting, Matthew has a quizzical look on his face, with his left hand pointing back to himself, as if to say, "you mean me?" In front of him are the coins of his trade, and around him his colleagues. He leaves it all to follow the mysterious figure from Galilee.

When others complain about the poor quality of Jesus's choice, he offers the explanation that is so telling: Just as the sick need a doctor, so do sinners need a savior. Jesus chooses those most in need of his mercy precisely because they are most ready to respond to the invitation without question. We are all touched by God's mercy. In fact, only God's mercy allows us to respond to God's gracious invitation. We say, do we not, just before receiving communion, "Lord, I am not worthy that you should enter under my roof; but only say the word and my soul shall be healed"? None of us is worthy of the call, but the call comes nonetheless.

QUESTION: How is the Lord calling me today? How willing am I to respond to this call?

2

THE FIRST WEEK
OF LENT

THE FIRST SUNDAY, YEAR A

THEME: Blame Adam?

READINGS: Gen 2:7–9; 3:1–7; Ps 51; Rom 5:12–19 or 5:12, 17–19; Matt 4:1–11

"Do not put the Lord your God to the test" (Matt 4:7; Deut 6:16).

REFLECTION: St. Paul is the first New Testament author to connect the figure of Adam, the first man, with Jesus, whom he calls "the last Adam" (1 Cor 15:45). Today's second reading makes the connection explicit. Adam, humanity's oldest ancestor, sinned. Jesus overcomes that sin by his obedience to his heavenly Father. Paul calls Adam "the type of the one who was to come" (Rom 5:14). At the outset of Lent, we acknowledge our innate proclivity to sin. We also express our confidence in Jesus, who by his cross and resurrection opened a path for us to cure our sinfulness.

In the story of Adam and Eve, as recalled in today's first reading from Genesis, they get the credit for bringing sin and death into the world (nice going, ancestors!). But why should Adam and Eve get the blame for *our* sins? Don't we also have some responsibility? Having just begun Lent, we are reminded that human nature is unfortunately rooted in the desire to be like God, which was Adam and Eve's original temptation. Tricked by the wily serpent, they think they can become the Creator, even though they are merely creatures. Is not this truly an "original sin"? Don't we all desire somehow to rule our own lives, to be omnipotent, to be like God?

The gospel reading today is Matthew's version of the temptation narrative. It shows that Jesus, as a human being like us, also could be tempted. The concept of temptation in Greek (*peirasmos*) is more properly described as a testing. Satan, not in the guise of a serpent this time, truly tests Jesus as "the Son of God." He tries three times to get Jesus to succumb. In other words, he tries to get him to act like Adam. Jesus is, after all, God's Son. Can't he free himself from his Father and be his own man? Each time, Jesus responds to the tempter's demand with words from the Book of Deuteronomy. He spars with the devil, who also knows how to quote Scripture. Yet Jesus does not surrender. Unlike Adam, he does not yield to the test. He remains faithful to his identity as God's true, obedient Son, unlike Adam. This is the model he provides for us on this First Sunday of Lent. We are called to place our Adam-like, innate human tendency to sin, in abeyance.

QUESTION: How can I improve my ability to resist the kinds of temptations that come my way?

THE FIRST SUNDAY, YEAR B

THEME: Over the Rainbow

READINGS: Gen 9:8–15; Ps 25; 1 Pet 3:18–22; Mark 1:12–15

"I set my bow in the clouds to serve as a sign of the covenant between me and the earth" (Gen 9:13).

REFLECTION: Numerous waterfalls bear the name Rainbow Falls. One lesser known one is found in the Ansel Adams Wilderness near

Mammoth Lakes, California. The hike to Rainbow Falls is a favorite one because even on the hottest, sunniest days, you are virtually guaranteed to see a colorful rainbow at the falls due to the interplay of the mist off the falls and sunshine. Who doesn't like a rainbow? Not only is it colorful, but it speaks of storms winding down, calm weather returning, and hopefulness.

Human beings have likely marveled at rainbows since time immemorial. Little wonder that Genesis, in today's first reading, records the rainbow as a sign of God's new covenant with Noah after the catastrophic flood that destroyed sinful humanity. God wanted to start over again. He focused on Noah and his family because they were representative of those humans willing to try to be faithful to God's covenant. The rainbow is intended for "every mortal being" (Gen 9:15, 16). Everyone is included. Everyone is invited to appreciate this hopeful sign. Maybe, just maybe, we can resist temptation and live as God desires.

Today's gospel reading connects with this hopeful plan. It narrates Mark's version of Jesus's temptation in the wilderness, which is much shorter than either Matthew's or Luke's versions. It simply says that the Spirit drove Jesus into the desert, where Satan tempted him for forty days and where he was "among wild beasts" (Mark 1:13). No rainbows here. The curious mention of the wild beasts may imply the risks of being in wild areas. Ancient peoples thought of the desert or wilderness as the abode of demons. It was dangerous, a place to avoid. Jesus, however, returns victorious, equipped to launch his ministry of proclaiming the good news of God's kingdom. This mission also involves repentance; it includes the call to "believe in the gospel" (Mark 1:15). In short, on this First Sunday of Lent, we resolve to repent and reform our lives. This is not a search for "somewhere over the rainbow." It is rather an opportunity to follow the Holy Spirit's lead and move forward in our lives of faith.

QUESTION: If I am ever tempted to lose hope in my ability to reform my life, how does my faith in God help?

21

THE FIRST SUNDAY, YEAR C

THEME: The Testing

READINGS: Deut 26:4–10; Ps 91; Rom 10:8–13; Luke 4:1–13

"When the devil had finished every temptation, he departed from him for a time" (Luke 4:13).

REFLECTION: As children, my siblings and I were urged by our parents to decide what sacrifices we were going to make throughout Lent. We were told to abstain from something we really liked (dessert, candy!), and also to set aside money from our weekly allowances for the poor (Operation Rice Bowl and other coin-collecting ventures). We were sternly warned not to give in to temptations that would inevitably arrive. If we did well and avoided temptations, our Lent would be fruitful and our Easter all the more wonderful.

It sounds simple, doesn't it? Just avoid temptation. The problem, however, is that we have domesticated what the Gospels mean by temptation. Does it not seem a bit exaggerated when today's gospel reading claims that the devil had finished *every* temptation against Jesus? Really? All temptations during the forty days in the wilderness? Even more curious is the assertion that the devil left Jesus "for a time." Why? Because the devil will be back. Only in Luke does the devil return (now called Satan) at the beginning of the passion narrative to seduce Judas to betray his Master (22:3) and to lead the disciples away (Luke 22:31). The devil never gives up.

What we might miss, though, is that this is not about "temptation" in the sense of being enticed to give in to one's simple desires. The Greek word actually means "testing." It conveys the sense of hardcore testing such as excessive athletic training to the point of exhaustion or being tortured. It is a real trial or ordeal, not a mere enticement. That is why Jesus teaches his disciples to pray not to be subjected to the "final test" (Luke 11:4). The concept behind this *test* is the apocalyptic woes that many Jews thought would precede the coming of the Messiah. It was envisioned as a time of terrible torment and anxiety.

This explanation helps us understand the deeper motivation for making Lenten resolutions. More important than setting limits to our preferred way of living on a daily basis is the challenge to perfect our prayer. We need to ask the Lord for strength when true testing comes our way. Will we be courageous enough to resist in the face of intense pressure?

QUESTION: In what ways am I "tested" in my life? What gives me courage to go on?

MONDAY OF THE FIRST WEEK

THEME: The Reckoning

READINGS: Lev 19:1–2, 11–18; Ps 19; Matt 25:31–46

"And he will separate them one from another, as a shepherd separates the sheep from the goats" (Matt 25:32).

REFLECTION: One of my worst memories from high school was of an elderly English literature teacher who was known to be very demanding. She warned students from the beginning of the year that she was indeed strict, but fair. She had high expectations, she said. As she distributed the first examination, she quipped, "Now class, remember, this too shall pass! You may not, but this examination will." I doubt that I was the only one who took a deep breath and waded into the exam with trepidation. Fortunately, my outcome was good. But it was not so with everyone.

Today's gospel reading is the famous judgment scene of the sheep and the goats. Unique to Matthew's Gospel, this reading is in synch with other passages from this same Gospel that threaten doom for those who do not act righteously (see 7:13; 8:12; 12:36–37; 22:13–14; etc.). Jesus in Matthew's Gospel sets the bar high. He calls for "the greater righteousness" (5:20). This is not a mere pious concept.

Acting righteously means treating our neighbors, our fellow human beings, according to God's will.

In accord with much of apocalyptic Judaism of his day, Jesus thought that there would eventually come a day of judgment. Ultimately, all human beings would be called before the judge to account for what we did or did not do in this life. Consider it a final examination of conscience, but one with important consequences. You either pass or fail. You either go to the eternal fires or to the kingdom of heaven. The criteria are concretely what we now term the corporal works of mercy: feeding the hungry, sheltering the homeless, welcoming immigrants and strangers, clothing the naked, visiting prisoners and those in nursing homes, and so on. Most surprising of all, we may not even recognize that what we did "to the least brothers [and sisters] of mine" we were doing for Christ himself.

My hunch is that everyone would like to pass their final (spiritual) exam! We all want to be sheep; no one wants to be a goat. Ultimately, however, when the judgment comes, the question is whether we will be prepared to answer for what we did or did not do with what God bestowed on us in this life. This message in Matthew is not meant to be merely a warning. This is not "Santa Claus religion"— "you better watch out"; rather, it is a call to stand up for truth, righteousness, and goodness in the midst of daily life. Part of our Lenten journey is to be prepared for just such an evaluation.

QUESTION: What are my priorities as a Christian? Do they coincide with the criteria expressed by Jesus in Matthew 25?

TUESDAY OF THE FIRST WEEK

THEME: Prayer from the Heart

READINGS: Isa 55:10–11; Ps 34; Matt 6:7–15

"In praying, do not babble like the pagans, who think they will be heard because of their many words" (Matt 6:7).

REFLECTION: One time while attending a wedding reception as a guest, a minister was invited to do the blessing before the meal. While he droned on and on and on, I could see guests beginning to fidget nervously. The soup was already served and getting cold. You could see eyes rolling, and almost hear the suppressed sighs. Enough already! Can we sit down and eat?

Of course, not just clergy sometimes go overboard in wordy prayers or statements. Anyone might succumb to this practice. The Greek word translated as "babble," in fact, means someone who stammers, like a baby making sounds but not really communicating. What is comforting, however, as we proceed on our Lenten pilgrimage, is to know that it is not the length or articulation of our prayers that counts. Jesus, in today's gospel reading instead instructs his followers to pray simply and from the heart. This passage occurs right in the center of the Sermon on the Mount (Matt 5—7). In contrast to longwinded, elegant prayers, Jesus says simply: "This is how you are to pray: Our Father in heaven…" (Matt 6:9). We know this as "the Lord's prayer." In reality, it might be better termed "the disciples' prayer." Jesus taught it to his followers. In doing so, he shared his intimate relationship with his heavenly Father, whom he tenderly addressed as "Abba, Father" (Mark 14:36).

While this prayer seems simple—indeed, children memorize it easily—have you noticed how artfully constructed it is? The first three phrases focus on God and God's kingdom: holy be your name, your kingdom come, your will be done. The remaining phrases focus on us: give us daily bread, forgive our debts as we forgive our debtors, don't allow us to be tempted, and deliver us from evil. This prayer expresses perfectly the vertical and horizontal dimensions of our faith. It is reminiscent of Jesus putting together the great Jewish Shema Yisrael prayer ("Hear, O Israel," Deut 6:4) to love God with your whole being, and the command to love your neighbor as yourself (Lev 19:18) in the two greatest commandments (Matt 22:37–40). What counts in prayer is this: we open ourselves fully to God

25

and to our neighbor. We pray simply yet profoundly both in word and, more importantly, in sentiment, from the depths of our being.

QUESTION: What is the quality of my prayer life? Do I pray simply and sincerely from the heart?

WEDNESDAY OF THE FIRST WEEK

THEME: The Double Surprise

READINGS: Jonah 3:1–10; Ps 51; Luke 11:29–32

"Who knows? God may again repent and turn from his blazing wrath, so that we will not perish" (Jonah 3:9).

REFLECTION: Who does not like nice surprises? If it is a double surprise, it might even be called a "win-win" situation. This is just what we find in today's Lenten readings, oriented especially toward the prophet Jonah.

The Book of Jonah is a beloved book in the Old Testament. It tells the story of a reluctant prophet whom God directs to go to Nineveh, the capital city of Israel's archenemy Assyria in the eighth century BCE. God tells Jonah to go preach a message of repentance to Nineveh, but Jonah instead flees, taking a ship in the opposite direction. A huge storm arises, and when Jonah admits he is likely the cause of the storm, the sailors throw him overboard. A great fish (not a whale) comes and swallows Jonah, who remains three days in its belly. Then it spits Jonah out on land, and he proceeds with his mission.

Then comes the first surprise. After only one day of preaching repentance and barely covering a third of the huge city, the Ninevites put on sackcloth, begin a fast, and repent! They express hope that the God of Israel might relent in punishing them, as stated in the excerpt above. The text even states that all the city, from the king to the cattle, repented! This is not what Jonah was expecting. He was looking forward to some fireworks from God. He was hoping for fire and brimstone.

Then comes the second, and even more startling, surprise. The climax of today's reading announces succinctly: "When God saw by their actions how they turned from their evil way, he repented of the evil he had threatened to do to them; he did not carry it out" (Jonah 3:10). A double surprise! The sinners repent and God relents. That is indeed the message of conversion. In today's gospel reading, Jesus reminds his hearers of "the sign of Jonah" and the surprising results of his preaching. He notes, however, that there is one greater than Jonah present to them. After three days in the tomb, he will rise from the dead, a most surprising development indeed.

Note, too, that Psalm 51 appears once more in today's readings. The quintessential penitential psalm follows the first reading as a reminder that we, like King David, should acknowledge our sinfulness and seek forgiveness. As Christians, we should never be surprised at God's broad and deep mercy, but we must make the first step of trusting in it by our humble acknowledgment of sin.

QUESTION: How much confidence do you have that God can forgive whatever sins you may have on your conscience?

THURSDAY OF THE FIRST WEEK

THEME: Ask, Seek, Knock

READINGS: Esther C:12, 14–16, 23–25; Ps 138; Matt 7:7–12

"Save us by your power, and help me, who am alone and have no one but you, Lord" (Esth C 25).

REFLECTION: As I have grown older and more reflective of my life, I have realized that sometimes I have been too timid. Whether asking my parents for permission to go on a camping trip with friends or requesting assistance from a math teacher to help solve some tough problems, I often stayed silent. I was afraid of hearing the answer I did not want—No! Both readings in today's liturgy indicate why being timid is not a gospel value (not to be confused with being humble!).

The Book of Esther is a fascinating tale that exists in two different versions, one in Hebrew and one in Greek.[1] It tells the tale of a heroine loosely based on the time when the Jewish people were under the authority of the Persian Empire (fifth century BCE). The heroine, Queen Esther, boldly does everything she can to save her Jewish people from evil forces bent on their destruction. Today's text is an excerpt from her eloquent prayer to God to save the people and help her in her loneliness. She feels utterly abandoned, yet she boldly asks God to intervene.

Esther provides a proper model for Jesus's teaching in today's gospel reading. It comes from the Sermon on the Mount. Jesus instructs his followers in clear language: "Ask and it will be given to you; seek and you will find; knock and the door will be opened to you" (Matt 7:7). Jesus encourages his disciples to be bold in their prayer. Don't hesitate to ask; don't hesitate to plead; don't hesitate to seek help when you most need it. Jesus likens his heavenly Father to much more than a human parent who knows how to give good things to his children.

To be sure, caution is needed to understand this message. These biblical passages assure us that God does hear and answer prayers. We are truly urged to ask, to seek, to knock on the door. But nothing promises that the way these prayers will be answered will necessarily be in the form that *we* want. We are not the ones who know what is best for us. That is God's business. This should not, however, stop our prayers. Be bold, says Jesus, and let your heavenly Father respond with wisdom.

QUESTION: Have you ever felt alone with no one to aid you? If so, how did you cope? Does your faith in God alone sustain you?

---

1. In the Book of Esther, the use of the letters *A* through *F* indicate the Greek elements of the story, while the customary chapter and verse numbers represent the Hebrew version.

FRIDAY OF THE FIRST WEEK

THEME: The Greater Righteousness

READINGS: Ezek 18:21–28; Ps 130; Matt 5:20–26

"I tell you, unless your righteousness surpasses that of the scribes and Pharisees, you will not enter into the kingdom of heaven" (Matt 5:20).

REFLECTION: As a teacher, I once had a student who was rather brash and bold. He approached me privately after the course had begun to inquire what was the least he could do to get a passing grade. He basically admitted he was not interested in learning anything. This was a required course; so, what did he have to do to scrape by and fulfill his obligation? As you might imagine, I was not impressed with his request. But at least he was honest.

Today's gospel reading cites another excerpt from the Sermon on the Mount. This Sermon is the boldest ethical statement of Jesus in the Gospels. To this day, it serves as a centerpiece in the ethical teaching of the *Catechism of the Catholic Church*. Jesus apparently was not a minimalist, as is evident from the citation above. He called his disciples to a *maximalist* ethic, the *greater* righteousness. This becomes even more apparent in the next section of the Sermon called "antitheses"—"you have heard it said, but I say to you…" (Matt 5:21–48)—where Jesus demands more of his disciples than is usually expected.

Let's be clear, though, that this is not an anti-Jewish trope. The Pharisees, in fact, were a pious lay group whose desire was to make the Torah or law more easily lived among the common people. They believed in an oral interpretation of the law, not only the written law. Later in Matthew, Jesus even reminds his hearers to honor the teachings of the scribes and Pharisees because they have taken "their seat on the chair of Moses" (23:2). No, this is not about denigrating a religion. It is, however, about warning all people of *any religion* who would consider themselves holy and righteous, that if their actions do not match their words, then their righteousness is hollow. It is for show. It is hypocrisy; it is a sham.

How many scandals have we witnessed even in our own day of religious leaders who preached one thing and lived another? It is even worse when we seek to impose on others what we ourselves cannot live.

The call to the greater righteousness is a call to authentic discipleship. Lent is the season that provides us the opportunity to put this vision into practice. Ezekiel, in today's first reading, reminds us that God does not desire our destruction; rather, God asks us to live righteously, avoid sin, and turn from all sorts of wickedness, and thus prepare to receive God's reward on the day of judgment. To live righteously requires resisting the temptation to think of our religiosity in smug terms. It demands that we live the greater righteousness, the more, not the less.

QUESTION: How authentic is my commitment to live an ethically upright life in the light of the gospel of Jesus Christ? Am I open to going the extra mile, to doing more than the minimum?

SATURDAY OF THE FIRST WEEK

THEME: Be Perfect?

READINGS: Deut 26:16–19; Ps 119; Matt 5:43–48

"So be perfect, as your heavenly Father is perfect" (Matt 5:48).

REFLECTION: Excuse me, Jesus. Did I hear you correctly? You want *me* to be as perfect as your heavenly Father? Are you kidding? Do you not know that psychologists consider perfectionism a human defect? Perfectionists are really hard to live with. Maybe you have never met one, but I assure you, they are difficult people. Nothing ever suits them. They complain. They always see the cup half empty, never half full. They are never content with anything, even with their own condition. So, what gives? As I read the lives of many of the saints, they were hardly *perfect* people! I can try my best, of course, but being perfect seems out of the question.

This is what I would like to say to Jesus, if I had the courage. But as I reflect on the Gospel, I wonder if it would be necessary. The Greek word translated "perfect" is *teleios*. It does not mean perfect in the sense that we take it in English. It comes from a word group that means to accomplish, bring to completion, to mature, attain a goal, or be goal oriented. This is not the same as being without fault. As we well know, many saints had their flaws. Just read the correspondence between St. Augustine and St. Jerome, and you will get some juicy evidence of subtle jealousies and disagreements. Or read the homilies of St. John Chrysostom, one of the greatest preachers of antiquity, and cringe at his antisemitic remarks that are totally unacceptable today. Or consider St. Peter, who did not have the courage to stick with Jesus in his most difficult trial and who even denied that he knew him! These were not perfect people, yet they were great saints because they took the word of God seriously and tried to understand it in depth and live according to its mandates. When they failed, because they were not in fact perfect, they repented and sought forgiveness, but they remained goal oriented. They sought the kingdom of God earnestly.

Today's first reading explains Moses's call to the chosen people that reinforces this perspective, echoed by the response from Psalm 119: "Be careful, then, to observe them [all God's statutes] with all your heart and with all your soul" (Deut 26:16; Ps 119:2). It is all about pursuing the kingdom or reign of God with all that we are— body, heart, mind, and soul—in other words, our entire being. That is being "perfect" in the way God (and Jesus) intends.

QUESTION: The real question behind Jesus's call to perfection is: Am I truly goal oriented? Do I put the reign of God first in my life, so that all else will fall into place behind it?

3

THE SECOND WEEK
OF LENT

THE SECOND SUNDAY, YEAR A

THEME: The Journey Begins

READINGS: Gen 12:1–4a; Ps 33; 2 Tim 1:8b–10; Matt 17:1–9

"Go forth from your land" (Gen 12:1).

REFLECTION: It is often said that every journey begins with a single step. But put yourself in Abram's place in today's first reading. God simply tells him to go forth from his land, from his home, with all his family and possessions. He isn't even told where to go. The destination is some vague "land that I will show you." The next verse (4b), missing from the lectionary, explains that Abram (whose name will change to Abraham) was seventy-five years old when this happened! Wow! No wonder St. Paul used Abraham as his model for what faith is about: absolute, unquestioning trust in God (see Rom 4:3; Gal 3:6).

Our Lenten journey is not far advanced from Ash Wednesday. Yet on this Second Sunday of Lent we hear Matthew's version of the transfiguration of Jesus on a mountaintop. This amazing moment is witnessed by the inner circle of Jesus, namely Peter, James, and John, the sons of Zebedee. They witness future glory but without real comprehension of what it means. They are bowled over by Jesus's dazzling transformation before their eyes, and they want to stay on the mountain. Moses and Elijah—symbolic of the law and the prophets (Matt 5:17)—appear, conversing with Jesus. But then a voice from heaven booms out: "This is my beloved Son, with whom I am well pleased; listen to him." This event is merely a glimpse of the glory to come. First, however, the disciples have to descend from the mountain. They need to get back on the road. They cannot camp out on the mountaintop. Nor can they halt the journey to Jerusalem. They must still learn what Jesus's ministry is truly about. They must listen carefully to his message. He is the suffering Son of Man who will give his life as a ransom for all.

The message of this Lenten Sunday is that we must move on in our lives. There is no pause or resting on our laurels. Our destination is clear: we are bound for the glories of God's kingdom. But to arrive there, we have to continue our earthly pilgrimage. We, too, have to listen carefully to what Jesus teaches.

QUESTION: Where am I in my own spiritual journey? How can I maintain the stamina to continue, even when I may not see where the road is leading me?

THE SECOND SUNDAY, YEAR B

THEME: The Beloved Son

READINGS: Gen 22:1–2, 9a, 10–13, 15–18; Ps 116; Rom 8:31b–34; Mark 9:2–10

"This is my beloved Son. Listen to him" (Mark 9:7).

REFLECTION: Every year the Second Sunday of Lent tells the story of the transfiguration. This year's account from Mark is the most spartan of the three versions. While the focus of all three accounts is on Jesus as the "beloved Son," this year this theme becomes even more prominent because it is coupled with the Genesis story of the sacrifice of Isaac. Isaac was Abraham's only son with Sarah, his wife. Abraham was said to be one hundred years old when Isaac was born (Gen 21:5). Sarah wasn't much younger! To call this a miraculous birth would be an understatement, yet it is testimony to how God can work wonders when we least expect them.

From a faith perspective, this story of Isaac is intimately tied to the story of Jesus. Isaac is the prefigurement of Jesus. Both are the unique and beloved sons of their fathers. Both are paradoxically offered up as a sacrifice. In the first instance, although Abraham cannot fathom why this should be so, he does not question God's rationale or hesitate. Yet God stays his hand at the last minute and proffers a ram instead. As for Jesus, he also does not question or hesitate. If he prays in the garden of Gethsemane that he would prefer not to have to sacrifice his life (Mark 14:36), he nonetheless willingly offers himself. What we glimpse on this Second Sunday of Lent, though, is the future glory that will come to Jesus by way of the cross. His Father does not, in fact, abandon him. Jesus is vindicated by the resurrection. The transfiguration is the promise of future glory. This beloved Son will also be rewarded, albeit not with a substitute sacrifice but with new life that conquers both sin and death.

QUESTION: How appreciative am I of Jesus's identity as God's only begotten Son? How well do I listen to him, follow him?

THE SECOND SUNDAY, YEAR C

THEME: Metamorphosis

READINGS: Gen 15:5–12, 17–18; Ps 27; Phil 3:17—4:1 or 3:20—4:1; Luke 9:28b–36

"And behold, two men were conversing with him, Moses and Elijah, who appeared in glory and spoke of his exodus that he was going to accomplish in Jerusalem" (Luke 9:30–31).

REFLECTION: When she was in the first grade, one of my great-nieces approached me and asked, "Uncle Ron, do you want to see my chrysalis?" A first-grader! Talking about the cocoon of a butterfly. She then went on to explain what a chrysalis is and what would happen after a short time, when the insect inside the cocoon would suddenly burst forth and be born a beautiful butterfly. She saw it through to the end and delighted in the transformation. I was impressed.

Sometimes this reality of natural metamorphosis has been used as an explanation for the transfiguration of Jesus, always celebrated on the Second Sunday of Lent. In fact, the Greek verb *metamorphoō* is used in the versions of the transfiguration in Mark (9:2) and Matthew (17:2). It is a rare verb in the New Testament and generally means a "change of nature." But today's gospel reading from Luke does not use this word. Instead, Luke speaks of the face of Jesus being changed in appearance while he prayed. Then, when Moses and Elijah miraculously appear "in glory" with Jesus in this transformed state, they speak of his *departure*. Note that the Greek word is *exodos* (exodus), the same word used of God's most important salvific event for the chosen people, leading them out of bondage in Egypt to the promised land. This is God's quintessential act of salvation until the sending of his own Son, which is why it also figures prominently during Lent.

Luke's version of the transfiguration prepares for Jesus's most important journey, the pilgrimage to Jerusalem to meet his fate. It formally begins at Luke 9:51, when Jesus "sets his face" toward Jerusalem, an expression indicating the firm resolve of a prophet who knows his destiny. The transfiguration offers a brief moment on the road when the coming "glory" of Jesus is revealed. The visual reality is reinforced by a word from a cloud: "This is my chosen Son; listen to him!"

Why do we always use the transfiguration on the Second Sunday of Lent? After all, we have only completed a week and some days of Lent. There is a long way to go. We must recall, however, that although Lent is our penitential pilgrimage, we already know the final outcome of the story of Jesus. We know it ultimately leads to glory. Every Sunday is a mini-celebration of Easter. It is a day to recall the resurrection.

That is why the Sundays of Lent are technically outside the penitential season. We celebrate the mystery of the cross and resurrection every time we gather for the Eucharist. We know, by faith, that the transformation previewed by Jesus is a mystery. It cannot be explained rationally. St. Paul tries to explain it to the Philippians in today's second reading as Jesus changing our "lowly body to conform with his glorified body" (Phil 3:21). Today, we glimpse our future. Jesus, our Savior, does not leave us stranded. He promises to bring us along. We will share in this dramatic transformation that he already lives.

QUESTION: How can the Lord transform your life? Do you believe in the mysterious power of God's transformative grace?

MONDAY OF THE SECOND WEEK

THEME: Mercy without End

READINGS: Dan 9:4b–10; Ps 79; Luke 6:36–38

"Be merciful, just as your Father is merciful" (Luke 6:36).

REFLECTION: In my more honest moments with my spiritual director, I admit that I often struggle with keeping my urge to execute judgment against perceived wrongdoers in check. Justice seems to demand it, right? After all, if we let evildoers get away with it, won't they just continue to wallow in their depravity?

In 1983, I went to see a movie about a washed-up country music singer who finds redemption when a woman helps him turn his life around. I always liked the film's title: *Tender Mercies*. It was an award-winning film but not a box office success, so it quickly disappeared. Nevertheless, the title has haunted me these many years.

Tender mercies—this is what God's brand of justice is all about. It makes no sense from our perspective. But from God's point of view, everything encompasses God's rich and undeserved mercy.

The quotation from today's gospel reading is the Lukan version of Jesus's teaching about perfection that we heard last Saturday. In place of a sermon on a mountaintop, Luke describes Jesus's "sermon on the level ground" (6:20–49). The teaching about being merciful and not being judgmental comes in the middle of it. Mercy is a key theme in Luke's Gospel. Today's reading is also supported by the first reading from Daniel, which speaks of God's covenantal mercy toward us, despite our persistent tendency to sin. Psalm 79 echoes the same theme. The psalmist asks God not to judge us according to our sinfulness, what we deserve, but to disregard the iniquities of the past. Look upon us tenderly, Lord!

We should recall that there is a tie-in between mercy and not being judgmental. Mercy may not be deserved, but God freely offers it if we but acknowledge our sinfulness and seek to rectify our lives. Valerie Schultz, author of the highly original book *Overdue: A Dewey Decimal System of Grace*, put this mystery succinctly: "Grace is when God gives us something we do not deserve. Mercy is when God does *not* give us what we *do* deserve."[1]

Being merciful like God is not easy. It is, however, the demand of the good news of Jesus Christ. Jesus asks us to transcend our human desire to judge others by our standards and to look instead to God's measures. God's tender mercy, it seems, is without end.

QUESTION: What is the quality of my mercy? Do I keep my urge for judging others in check?

TUESDAY OF THE SECOND WEEK

THEME: Cleanse the Inside as Well as the Outside

READINGS: Isa 1:10, 16–20; Ps 50; Matt 23:1–12

"Wash yourselves clean!… / Though your sins be like scarlet, / they may become white as snow; / Though they be red like crimson, / they may become white as wool" (Isa 1:16, 18).

---

1. Valerie Schultz, "We Know the Feeling," *Give Us This Day* 14, no. 2 (Feb. 2024): 269–70, original emphases.

REFLECTION: Readers might recall an old folk saying that my parents would often cite for us children, especially before coming to sit at the dinner table: "Cleanliness is next to godliness. Go wash up!" As a boy, I certainly needed to wash up before sitting at table. Playing hard, whether in sports or just goofing off with friends on the lawn or in the nearby forest, we usually came home quite dirty.

Today's command from the prophet Isaiah, however, is not about physical washing. It is about cleansing ourselves from the inside out. Isaiah makes explicit the kind of "washing" we are to do: care for the oppressed, orphans, and widows (1:17). In other words, if we accomplish justice for the vulnerable and oppressed, our blood-red sins will be cleansed as white as snow. The Old Testament regularly exhorts the covenant people to care for the widow, the orphan, and the stranger. These are the "big three" of the most vulnerable in that society. They also are symbolic of all who are subject to oppression. Widows usually had no means of livelihood without their husbands. Orphans were often left destitute and had to scrape by with miserable lives in the street, and strangers were often mistrusted, shunned, or simply overlooked. Today, we might think of refugees and immigrants who are often despised and marginalized. The kind of cleansing God desires is that which promotes mercy and tenderness toward the vulnerable. When Jesus rails against the hypocrisy of some of the Jewish leaders in today's gospel reading, it is not a criticism of their authority or their interpretation of God's law. The lack of putting it into practice concretely is what provokes Jesus's righteous harangue.

I wonder if we cannot see another subtle meaning to Isaiah's exhortation to wash ourselves clean. Lent is a spiritual journey that ultimately leads us back to our baptismal promises. In fact, throughout Lent we accompany in prayer catechumens, those who are preparing to enter the family of faith through baptism. It is a spiritual washing that both takes away sin and inaugurates a new life, the life of faith in a community of the faithful. When Lent ends and the feast of the resurrection arrives, we will all renew our baptismal promises. We will once more invite the waters of baptism to flow over us, cleanse us inside out, and restore our right relationship with God and neighbor.

QUESTION: What parts of my spiritual or ethical way of living are in need of cleansing?

WEDNESDAY OF THE SECOND WEEK

THEME: The Cup

READINGS: Jer 18:18–20; Ps 31; Matt 20:17–28

"Can you drink the chalice that I am going to drink?" (Matt 20:22).

REFLECTION: What mother doesn't want the best for her children? The gospel reading today tells of an encounter between Jesus and the mother of James and John, the sons of Zebedee. These two disciples were clearly part of the inner circle of Jesus, along with Simon Peter. Only Matthew records this scene in which the mother of these two approaches Jesus, kneels before him, and implores him to honor her sons by placing them on his left and right. We should not miss that this scene comes directly after the third, and most explicit, passion prediction (Matt 20:17–19). So, the context should be clear. Jesus will have to suffer and be crucified. The image of Jeremiah, the suffering prophet, looms in the background, as seen in today's first reading. Still, the mother asks Jesus for this favor. He explains, however, that such positions are not his to give but remain with his heavenly Father.

Jesus's reply is telling. He asks the two disciples (not the mother!), "Can you [plural] drink the cup [in Greek, *potērion*] that I am going to drink?" The Greek word for "cup" (not "chalice," as in the lectionary translation) is important because it was a familiar Jewish metaphor for accepting one's fate, often death. Jesus tells the unnamed mother that she doesn't understand what she is asking. His question, however, is directed to the two disciples. Perhaps they are eagerly anticipating a positive answer. They are obviously seeking a privileged position, for when the other ten disciples hear of this exchange, they become angry. This leads to Jesus's explanation that they should not be grasping at such honors. They are not to be like the "the Gentiles" who lord it over one another. They are called to be servants to one another. Like Jesus himself, they are to serve and not be served. He is even "to give his life as a ransom for many" (20:28).

In Mark's version of this story, the two disciples ask for this honor themselves (Mark 10:35–45). Matthew's version maybe softens somewhat the picture of the ambitious disciples. Mom wanted the best for her sons, but I don't think she realized that what she was asking would jeopardize their very survival. The two disciples eagerly say yes to their willingness to drink the same cup as Jesus, but when confronted with that reality in the garden of Gethsemane, they flee, leaving Jesus to drink the cup alone.

QUESTION: How readily do we express our willingness to follow Jesus even unto death?

THURSDAY OF THE SECOND WEEK

THEME: Testing the Heart

READINGS: Jer 17:5–10; Ps 1; Luke 16:19–31

"More tortuous than anything is the human heart, / beyond remedy; / who can understand it? / I, the LORD, explore the mind and test the heart, / Giving to all according to their ways, / according to the fruit of their deeds" (Jer 17:9–10).

REFLECTION: Ancient Egypt continues to fascinate me. Even as a boy, I was intrigued by the images that came from ancient Egyptian culture. Think of the tremendous archaeological finds that came from King Tutankhamun's tomb. Several blockbuster art exhibits have drawn international attention to this fascinating ancient civilization.

One of the powerful preoccupations in ancient Egyptian culture concerned what happened after death. Egyptians believed that in order to pass to the afterlife, the heart of the deceased had to be placed on a scale before the eternal judge Osiris, to see if it was worthy. A true heart merited reward; an evil heart was denied an eternal reward. There was no escaping this judgment.

The prophet Jeremiah in today's first reading reveals a related understanding, albeit from a Hebrew mentality. Who can truly know the human heart? In Jewish anthropology, the heart was not the seat of emotions—those were found deep in the bowels of an individual—but the seat of wisdom, of justice, and of right judgments. To the mystery of the human heart, God uses Jeremiah's words to assert categorically that I, the Lord, know the human mind and heart! In the end, God will repay each person according to the "fruit" of their deeds.

Today's gospel reading picks up on this divine judgment through the story of Lazarus and the unnamed rich man, whom later tradition called Dives (Latin for "rich man"). For years the rich man had ignored this poor beggar at his door. But when death came for the two of them, Lazarus arrived to Abraham's bosom, while Dives went to eternal suffering. A just reward executed by a righteous God. There is no escape, no opportunity to backtrack in life. God knows our inmost being, the deepest recesses of our minds and hearts. Lent reminds us of the necessity to examine ourselves inwardly and see where we stack up to what God requires. Psalm 1 appears again in this regard, as the response to Jeremiah's reading. There are only two ways: God's ways in accordance with the law and the prophets, or human ways according to our selfish desires. This is not a threat nor a trite scenario. It is the way of faith.

QUESTION: Is my heart ready to be weighed on the scales of divine justice?

FRIDAY OF THE SECOND WEEK

THEME: The Hazards of Prophecy

READINGS: Gen 37:3–4, 12–13a, 17b–28a; Ps 105; Matt 21:33–43, 45–46

Jesus said to them, "Did you never read in the scriptures: 'The stone that the builders rejected / has become the cornerstone; / by the Lord has this been done, / and it is wonderful in our eyes'?" (Matt 21:42; see Ps 118:22–23).

REFLECTION: In my more fanciful moments, I have wondered about what a job description for a prophet might look like.

> Wanted: Someone with a strong voice, a firm sense of righteousness, and the ability to speak the truth no matter what the cost.
>
> Duties: Making people in authority and those with wealth uncomfortable; also the ability to perceive injustice and combat it.
>
> Wages: Meagre, with a prospect for being ostracized and martyred.
>
> Contact: Interested parties should inquire cautiously.

What is it that makes prophets do what they do? Sheer courage? Stubbornness? Why do such people make us uncomfortable? Jealousy? Fear of our true failures being revealed openly?

Today's readings speak to this situation forthrightly. In Jesus's parable of the tenants who usurp their master's vineyard, the tenants go so far as to kill the owner's son, thinking they will thereby inherit the property. This leads to Jesus's wry observation about the "stone the builders rejected" from Psalm 118. It foresees a reversal of fortune for the one initially rejected. He becomes the cornerstone. This is foreshadowed in the story of Joseph, the dreamer from the Book of Genesis (chapter 37). His brothers' jealousy laid him low for a time and nearly snuffed out his life, but he paradoxically prospered in Pharaoh's Egypt. The psalm response describes it deftly: "They shackled his feet with chains; / collared his neck in iron, / Till his prediction came to pass, / and the word of the LORD proved him true" (Ps 105:18–19). He was sold into slavery yet emerged triumphant.

Joseph, of course, was not a prophet. He was a beloved son who prefigured Jesus, the beloved son of his heavenly Father. According to Matthew, perhaps with some exaggeration, Israel had a habit of treating its prophets badly. In his lament over Jerusalem, the city of his own fate, Jesus cries out: "Jerusalem, Jerusalem, you who kill the prophets and stone those sent to you" (Matt 23:37).

It turns out that my fantasy about a prophet's job description is unwarranted. True prophets are not self-appointed. They don't seek the job. Instead, like Jonah, they flee from it. Or like Amos, they deny their prophetic pedigree. In the end, others are the ones who recognize true prophets, and usually after their fate has been sealed. Think of Abraham Lincoln, Martin Luther King Jr., and Mohandas Ghandi.

QUESTION: Who are the true prophets of our day? Who are the false prophets? How do we view them?

SATURDAY OF THE SECOND WEEK

THEME: Prodigal Mercy

READINGS: Micah 7:14–15, 18–20; Ps 103; Luke 15:1–3, 11–32

"I shall get up and go to my father and I shall say to him, 'Father, I have sinned against heaven and against you. I no longer deserve to be called your son'" (Luke 15:18–19).

REFLECTION: A favorite pastime of mine is to visit museums, especially art museums. During many years in Paris, I attended a host of special art exhibits, and not simply at the Louvre. One time, I came across a special exposition of paintings by James Tissot (1836–1902), a famous French artist most known for a series of paintings he did to illustrate an edition of the Bible. Many are held by the Brooklyn Museum.

What struck me about this small, special exposition, however, was the number of versions of the Prodigal Son Tissot painted. Some were set in ancient biblical times, others transposed to modern late nineteenth-century settings. What they all held in common, seen when exhibited side by side, was the remorse on the son's face and the joy on the father's when he returned. Apparently, Tissot saw himself as the recipient of unwarranted forgiveness in the face of some of his own bad life decisions. He kept playing the scene out over and over again.

In today's parable, the contrast between the two sons could not be more striking. The younger son, who insulted his father by taking his inheritance early and leading a profligate life, finally comes to his senses (v. 17; literally, "came to himself") and repents. He returns to his father, no longer expecting to be welcomed back as a son— his insensitive action had virtually rendered his father "dead"—but simply as a hired hand. Imagine his surprise when his father comes rushing out to embrace him and treats him like a prince, despite his disreputable behavior. The reaction of the older son, alas, is less salutary. His anger explodes, thinking that this gracious action on his father's part is unjust to him. He feels slighted and no doubt jealous. In the face of his father's seemingly prodigal mercy, all he can think about is himself. In fact, we might say, in contrast to his younger brother, this older brother never went outside himself! He therefore cannot accept his father's joy over this profligate son's return. When today's psalm response proclaims, "The LORD is kind and merciful," it places the emphasis not on the righteous judgment we deserve when we "go off the rails," but the joyous welcome we receive when we get back on the right track. That is what Lent should be about.

QUESTION: Have I ever been the recipient of prodigal mercy? Do I rejoice when mercy comes to others?

4

THE THIRD WEEK OF LENT

THE THIRD SUNDAY, YEAR A

THEME: The Samaritan Woman and Living Water

READINGS: Exod 17:3–7; Ps 95; Rom 5:1–2, 5–8; John 4:5–42 or [shorter version] 4:5–15, 19b–26, 39a, 40–42

"The water I shall give will become in [that person] a spring of water welling up to eternal life" (John 4:14b).

REFLECTION: Every human being knows the precious commodity of water. No H_2O, no life. That is why some regions of the world, including parts of the United States, are worried. Changing weather patterns have sometimes led to dire droughts. Lakes have disappeared, reservoirs have dried up, and water for both drinking and irrigation is in desperately short supply. I can remember myself living through a seven-year drought in California. We were all encouraged to take three-minute showers (Navy showers!), and not necessarily every day.

I can sympathize with the plea of the Israelites in the desert for Moses to give them water. Although I have never truly been deprived of water, some areas of the world, especially during times of war, have indeed been bone dry. So, God answers the Israel-ites' prayer with miraculous "water from the rock." This miracle is symbolic of God's ability to quench the deepest human thirsts. Today's gospel reading is particularly appropriate for the initia-tion process of those preparing for baptism at the Easter Vigil or on Easter Sunday.

The Samaritan woman in today's gospel reading faces an entirely different situation. She is at the well-known Jacob's well and has come at the hottest time of the day to get water. Behold, a Jewish man amazingly asks for a drink. This leads to an exten-sive dialogue. Jesus promises her "living water," which is a double entendre meaning running water and water for eternal life.

This is the perfect story for the first of the three central Sun-days of Lent because it focuses on the basic element for baptism: water. Water cleanses, irrigates, fructifies, refreshes, and quenches thirst. Baptism by water and the Holy Spirit gives a new kind of life. To borrow a term from St. Paul, in the waters of baptism "into Christ" we become a "new creation" (Gal 3:28). The old is washed away, the new takes hold of us. This spiritual cleansing makes us new persons. It breaks down barriers and brings people into a new relationship. This is what Jesus did for the Samaritan woman who eventually came to confess her faith in Jesus. This is what God continues to do for people seeking to enter the family of God by baptism. Today is a proper day to rejoice in those who, during the scrutinies, profess their desire to slake their thirst with this holy water. Let us pray for them, support them, and welcome them with open arms.

QUESTION: How important is it for you to recall your own bap-tism in Christ Jesus? Do you bring it to consciousness when you come to church to worship with fellow believers?

46

THE THIRD SUNDAY, YEAR B

THEME: Scandal and Folly

READINGS: Exod 20:1–17; Ps 19; 1 Cor 1:22–25; John 2:14–21

"But we proclaim Christ crucified, a stumbling block to Jews and foolishness to Gentiles" (1 Cor 1:23).

REFLECTION: The word *scandal* likely evokes disgrace or shame. Politicians and other people in leadership positions often will do whatever they can to avoid any hint of scandal, for fear it will damage their reputation. The origin of the word in Greek (*skandalon*), however, really means "stumbling block," as in today's second reading from 1 Corinthians. It is something that trips us up, that serves more as a roadblock than a highway. Paul explains why neither Gentiles (Greeks) nor Jews can accept the main proclamation of the Christian faith. The cross makes no sense in human terms. It is a stumbling block and foolishness. Paul declares that "Jews demand signs and Greeks look for wisdom." The cross of Christ with which we began our Lenten journey satisfies neither preference. Yet that is the essence of Christianity—the cross and resurrection. The cross was the paradoxical instrument of our salvation. The resurrection was its vindication, the promise of new and eternal life.

While the Exodus reading about the Ten Commandments and the gospel reading about Jesus's cleansing of the temple provide good resources for reflection at this near midpoint in the Lenten season, focusing on the cross is also important. We likely wear crosses around our neck or pin them to our suits or blouses, but they are more than a decoration. The cross is the most profound and paradoxical symbol of how deeply God has loved us. For those who have faith, the cross is not a stumbling block. We begin and end each liturgy with the Sign of the Cross, and our prayers usually use the same gesture.

Perhaps it would be worthwhile to reflect more deeply on how we can make this simple, common gesture more an essential part of our identity.

QUESTION: How can I explain to others what the cross of Christ means, to me and to those who share my faith?

THE THIRD SUNDAY, YEAR C

THEME: Three Strikes

READINGS: Exod 3:1–8a, 13–15; Ps 103; 1 Cor 10:1–6, 10–12; Luke 13:1–9

"Sir, leave it for this year also, and I shall cultivate the ground around it and fertilize it; it may bear fruit in the future. If not, you can cut it down" (Luke 13:8–9).

REFLECTION: In the United States, at least, this time of the year baseball fans await with ardent anticipation the start of the baseball season. Spring training is underway, and opening day is not far off. Baseball has also given a common rule to human interactions: three strikes and you're out!

I am no expert on how the rules of baseball came into being. I do know, however, that already in antiquity there was a fairly common understanding of "the rule of three." Whether it had to do with stories, or jokes, or literary illustrations, the rule of three predominated. One or two items are not sufficient; four is too many. Three is just right. It's a figure that seems generous enough without overdoing it.

Surprise! In God's rule book, the rule of three can be bent. Take today's gospel reading. In a passage unique to Luke, Jesus offers two illustrations of one of his favorite themes—the call to repentance. The second of the two is about a barren fig tree. The owner obviously wants fruit. (Why else have a fig tree?) He tries for three successive years without success. So, he orders the gardener to cut it down. "Why should it exhaust the soil?" (v. 7b). The gardener makes a counteroffer. Sure, three years should be sufficient; three strikes and you should be out. But give it just one more chance. Maybe a little more cultivation and fertilizing will work. If that doesn't work, then cut it down.

The lesson is clear. God is like the gardener who gives a barren tree one more chance to fulfill its mission. Bear some fruit—a standard biblical image for living a righteous life—and you will live. The divine gardener makes an offer beyond the norm.

QUESTION: How many times have I been forgiven? How generous am I in extending forgiveness to others who have offended me?

MONDAY OF THE THIRD WEEK[1]

THEME: What Can Quench My Thirst?

READINGS: 2 Kgs 5:1–15b; Ps 42; Luke 4:24–30

"Athirst is my soul for the living God" (Ps 42:3).

REFLECTION: Paris is apparently still the number one vacation destination for American tourists, even more than London or Rome. Anyone who has been to Paris in summer, though, has likely experienced those rare super-hot days when you really work up a thirst while touring the city. Since few places are air-conditioned, at least in the manner to which we Americans are accustomed, you can have trouble finding an adequate place to cool off. Sometimes the best bet is simply to find an outdoor cafe, sit down, and order a cold, refreshing drink. The pause that refreshes—before you get thirsty again.

Today's theme makes an appropriate continuation in Year A of the theme of living water. It is also appropriate to Year B when the story of Naaman the Syrian features in the first reading and the gospel. Naaman the leper is a sign of God's healing power. Jesus

---

1. The following readings may be used on any day this week, especially in Years B and C when the gospel of the Samaritan woman is not read on the Third Sunday of Lent: Exod 17:1–7; Ps 95; John 4:5–42.

emphasizes that Naaman, an outsider in Jewish eyes, was the recipient of God's merciful outreach when he was instructed to immerse himself seven times (the perfect number!) in the Jordan River to be healed of his leprosy. Despite his skepticism, he fulfills the demand and is indeed cured.

So, the question in today's theme should not be "*what* can quench my thirst?" but *who*? The psalmist cries out, "As the hind longs for the running waters, / so my soul longs for you, O God. / Athirst is my soul for God, the living God. / When shall I go and behold the face of God?" (Ps 42:2–3).

God is not some temporary thirst quencher. God is not merely there for partial respite from the burning sun or a dry mouth. God is the *living* God, the one who can provide more fully every need in our lives. If we were truly honest with ourselves, we could see that our true spiritual thirst is for someone who loves us unconditionally. Someone in whom we can place our absolute trust. Someone whose constancy is assured.

QUESTION: Am I willing to place all my trust in God, the living God, who can truly quench all the "thirsts" of my life?

TUESDAY OF THE THIRD WEEK

THEME: Forgiveness Unlimited

READINGS: Dan 3:25, 34–43; Ps 25; Matt 18:21–35

"Lord, if my brother sins against me, how often must I forgive him? As many as seven times?" (Matt 18:21).

REFLECTION: Many of us probably like to think of ourselves as patient people. Not too quick to cast aspersions on someone. Perhaps willing to overlook faults or errors and think the best of individuals. Peter likely saw his question to Jesus in today's gospel reading as a very generous offer on his part. "As many as seven times?" Remembering that the number *seven* was considered the perfect number in the biblical perspective, Peter's offer seems very generous indeed. Yet Jesus's own response to the question is incredible: "I say to you, not seven times but seventy-seven times" (18:22). This multiplication of sevens basically means an infinite number of times! It is forgiveness without limit. To illustrate his point, Jesus goes on to tell the parable of the unmerciful servant, found only in Matthew's Gospel. The "king" forgives a servant his huge unpaid debt when he pleads for patience. But the wicked servant turns around and deals mercilessly with an underling who owes him a paltry amount. The one who received mercy was not willing to pass it on. The one who received undeserved patience was not willing to share the same.

From our human perspective, I suspect most of us lose patience at some point with individuals who time and again "sin" or perpetrate evil. Think of recidivism in criminals. Many are repeat offenders. Sometimes they even progress from lesser crimes to more serious ones. How patient, how forgiving, how merciful are we to be? Jesus concludes his lesson by saying that the heavenly Father will treat us sternly "unless each of you forgives your brother [or sister] from your heart" (verse 35). Heartfelt forgiveness is what Lent is about. We receive from the Lord what we are to pass on to others.

QUESTION: How can we apply Jesus's principle of limitless forgiveness in a real-world context where sin still abounds? How can we be merciful without fostering the evil we try to combat?

WEDNESDAY OF THE THIRD WEEK

THEME: Fulfilling Prophecy

READINGS: Deut 4:1, 5–9; Ps 147; Matt 5:17–19

"Do not think that I have come to abolish the law or the prophets. I have come not to abolish but to fulfill" (Matt 5:17).

REFLECTION: Have you ever wondered how prophecy works? How can you determine who is an authentic prophet and who is a phony? There have been many self-proclaimed prophets in history. Clearly, not all of them were the genuine item. Some led people astray; some tried to profit (pun intended!) from their alleged identity. What are we to think of Jesus's statement in the Sermon on the Mount from today's gospel reading? Do we not think that Jesus actually came to give a *new* law and that he surpassed what the prophets had foretold?

Actually, the problem of how to discern a true prophet is not new. Already in the Old Testament, in the same Book of Deuteronomy that describes God giving his whole law to the chosen people, we receive this advice:

> Should you say to yourselves, "How can we recognize that a
> word is one the LORD has not spoken?" If a prophet speaks
> in the name of the LORD but the word does not come true,
> it is a word the LORD did not speak. The prophet has spoken
> it presumptuously; do not fear him. (Deut 18:21–22)

This is tantamount to saying that we cannot really determine the authenticity of a prophetic word except by hindsight. In the meantime, we are placed in the uncomfortable position of having to believe whether a prophet is right or not. It all boils down to faith.

We believe now, of course, that Jesus Christ was indeed the Messiah and Son of God. We also accept that his words were true and still give life. What we should not miss in today's gospel reading, however, is that Jesus is not proclaiming a new law. Surprisingly, he says he is not abolishing the old law or the prophets but *fulfilling* them. How so? For Matthew, the response is that Jesus shows himself as the embodiment of the one and only law of God in word (the Sermon on the Mount, Matt 5—7) and in deed (the miracles, Matt 8—9). Jesus shows us that the law, which is summarized in the Ten Commandments (literally in Hebrew, "ten words") is not impossible. He shows the way. He shows us that doing God's will and heeding God's true prophets can lead us to the true life of faith.

Lent is essentially a return to the basics. No need to invent new rules or imagine novel spiritual exercises. Difficult though it might be to live God's law, it is not impossible.

QUESTION: What can I do to put into practice more profoundly the basics of God's law? How good am I at discerning right from wrong?

THURSDAY OF THE THIRD WEEK

THEME: A House Divided

READINGS: Jer 7:23–28; Ps 95; Luke 11:14–23

"Every kingdom divided against itself will be laid waste and house will fall against house" (Luke 11:17).

REFLECTION: As a Civil War buff, I enjoy reading about one of the true, great heroes who saved the Union, Abraham Lincoln. It was quite remarkable to hear Pope Francis invoke the figure of Lincoln (along with Dorothy Day, Thomas Merton, and Martin Luther King Jr.) when he addressed Congress on September 24, 2015. Lincoln is a fascinating individual from many different angles. One curious aspect is that he was not overtly religious. Although he attended church services from time to time, he read the Bible regularly and with care. The content and style of the Bible (King James version, to be sure) highly influenced his oratorical style.

One of Lincoln's most famous speeches was given on June 16, 1858, when he was a candidate for the Senate. The context obviously was the vexing question of slavery, which was creating deeper and deeper divisions in the country. Clearly drawing from Jesus's teaching in the Gospels, Lincoln spoke eloquently:

"A house divided against itself cannot stand." I believe this government cannot endure, permanently half *slave* and half *free*. I do not expect the Union to be *dissolved*—I do not expect the house to *fall*—but I *do* expect it will cease to be divided. It will become *all* one thing, or *all* the other.[2]

Some people suggest that we are currently living in the most divided times in U.S. and world history. Anecdotally, that may well be true. Yet looking back to mid-nineteenth-century America and Lincoln's context, they must have felt the same way. Division is sadly a part of the human condition, it seems. St. Paul had to deal with it in Corinth, for example, where factions were tearing apart the body of Christ (see 1 Cor 1:10–13). He chastised the Corinthians severely and called them back to their true identity as members of the undivided body of Christ.

Today's gospel reading reminds us that division is not to be a hallmark of disciples. Jesus rebuts his opponents' accusation that he works for Beelzebul, Satan. No kingdom, whether good or bad, can endure if divided. Neither can any community or nation or family or church. Living together is clearly not an easy task. It requires humility and self-sacrifice. It often requires compromise. But Jesus also warns us, "Whoever is not with me is against me, and whoever does not gather with me scatters" (Luke 11:23). We must *choose*. Do we want the one, or the other? Will we follow Satan, or God?

Ultimately, Lincoln gave his life for the sake of the entire nation. Ultimately, Jesus gave his life for the sake of the entire world. What are we doing to preserve unity rather than sowing the seeds of division?

QUESTION: What can we do in our own life situation to break down divisions in our world, our society, and our church to promote more lasting unity?

---

2. Abraham Lincoln, *Speeches and Writings, 1832–1858* (New York: Library of America, 1989), 426–32, here 426 (emphases original).

FRIDAY OF THE THIRD WEEK

THEME: Two Sides of the Same Coin

READINGS: Hos 14:2–10; Ps 81; Mark 12:28–34

"There is no other commandment greater than these [two]" (Mark 12:31).

REFLECTION: I was an avid reader of the *Peanuts* cartoons of Charles M. Shulz (1950–2000). I still find them enjoyable, though they are far less prevalent today than when I was growing up. One cartoon shows Linus being put down by his big sister Lucy. Lucy ridicules him for wanting to be a doctor because he does not have the capacity to love mankind [*sic*]. Linus, the "theologian" of the group of characters in the comic strip, exclaims, "I love mankind. It's people I can't stand."

Isn't that so often the case with us human beings? When it comes to generalities, we are fine. Tell me abstractly to love my neighbor, and doubtless most of us would agree. But when our neighbor in the flesh is someone who encroaches on our territory or has irksome habits suddenly looms in front of us, loving that person is much more difficult. Generalities are fine; particularities less so.

Today's gospel reading describes an encounter between Jesus and a scribe. We should not overlook that the context, unfortunately obscured by the editing of the lectionary, is one of controversy. The lectionary leaves out the modifying phrase, "heard them [certain scribes] disputing and saw how well he [Jesus] had answered them" (12:28 NABRE). This little detail is important, however, because this particular scribe approaches Jesus seemingly in a positive manner. He is not here to trap Jesus, unlike Jesus's enemies, who continue their devious tactics in the very next passage (12:35–37). The scribe reinforces his politeness by addressing Jesus as "Teacher" (12:32).

The scribe's question about which is the greatest commandment is not unique. In fact, in Jesus's day, this was a disputed question. And Jesus is not the only one to put together the two greatest commandments from Deut 6:4–5 and Lev 19:18—love of God with the whole of one's being, and love of neighbor as oneself. Other rabbis thought likewise. The first quotes the great Jewish prayer recited daily—the Shema Ysrael, "Hear, O Israel"—while the second connects love of God with love of neighbor, meaning love of other human beings. Nothing can compare to these two great commandments.

Pope Francis made an insightful comment on the combination of these two commandments, which sum up the whole of the law. He writes, "Even if set in a sequence, they are two sides of a single coin; experienced together they are a believer's strength!" He goes on to emphasize that "neighbor" here does not mean my preselected friend, but whomever I encounter on the journey of life.[3] Love of God and love of neighbor—two sides of the same coin. We cannot say that we love God and then detest our fellow human beings. That is Jesus's point. The two commandments are inseparable. You cannot generically love the invisible God and then detest the person next to you.

When the scribe rightly affirms Jesus in his response, Jesus replies that the scribe "is not far from the kingdom of God" (12:34). But being "not far" is not the same as being *in* the kingdom. The scribe is on the right path. But believers know that to go "all the way" with Jesus is to pick up your cross and follow (Mark 8:34). That's what we strive to do in Lent.

QUESTION: Do I honestly love God and neighbor in equal proportions? How can I grow in that love?

SATURDAY OF THE THIRD WEEK

THEME: Mercy, Not Sacrifices

READINGS: Hos 6:1–6; Ps 51; Luke 18:9–14

"For it is love that I desire, not sacrifice, and knowledge of God rather than burnt offerings" (Hos 6:6).

---

3. Pope Francis, *The Gospel of Mark: A Spiritual and Pastoral Reading* (Maryknoll, NY: Orbis, 2020), 189.

REFLECTION: Have you ever tried to bargain with God? Maybe, you've said something like, "Look, God, if you will only do such and such for me, I will do such and such to honor you." Maybe make sacrifices, give up favorite foods or drinks for a time, or go to church more regularly. Bargaining is like that. You scratch my back, I'll scratch yours. Do me a favor, and I'll do one for you.

In antiquity, many ancient religions were built upon the very notion of sacrifice. Although the root idea comes from a Latin word meaning "make holy," many ancient peoples thought the gods (or for Israel, God) demanded sacrifices. For Israel, this usually meant animal sacrifices offered at the altar in the temple, or perhaps agricultural offerings, like the first grains or fruits of the harvest. Making sacrifices ensured a right relationship with God and was presumed to bring God's blessing and prosperity.

The problem with this scenario is that some prophets, like Hosea, realized that reducing holiness to "burnt offerings" and religious rituals was not really what God desired, although they are a part of proper religious piety. More important to Israel's faith was supposed to be an inner devotion characteristic of a repentant heart. One's actions toward others were seen as a mirror of a proper interior disposition. Today's psalm response expresses it as well: "For you are not pleased with sacrifices; / should I offer a burnt offering, O God, you would not accept it. / My sacrifice, O God, is a contrite spirit; / a contrite, humbled heart, O God, you will not spurn" (Ps 51:18–19).

In Matthew's Gospel, Jesus makes a strong point in favor of this stance. He twice repeats the line from Hosea about the insufficiency of sacrifices and the primacy of love. When he is criticized by some Jewish leaders for hanging out with sinners, Jesus replies, "Go and learn the meaning of the words, 'I desire mercy, not sacrifice.' I did not come to call the righteous but sinners" (Matt 9:13; also 12:7). But we should note something important here. The word "mercy" is replaced by "love" in the first reading today. Why? The original Hebrew text, in fact, uses the expression "faithful, covenantal love" (in Hebrew, *chesed*). The Greek translation of the text (the Septuagint), however, employs the word "mercy" (in Greek, *eleos*). Different English translations follow one expression or the other. More to the point is that both mercy and love are characteristic of God's attitude toward humanity. They are also what God expects from all who would accept God's law. We do not need to worry about how to bargain with God. If we act out of a priority of love and mercy toward those around us, we will not need to be anxious about how God will view us. This does not mean abandoning all ritual. Rather, it means knowing where the priorities of our lives should be centered if we want to be more Godlike.

QUESTION: In what ways are mercy and love related concepts? Are they a priority in my life?

5

THE FOURTH WEEK OF LENT

THE FOURTH SUNDAY, YEAR A

THEME: The Man Born Blind and the Light

READINGS: 1 Sam 16:1b, 6–7, 10–13a; Ps 23; Eph 5:8–14; John 9:1–41 or [shorter version] 9:1, 6–9, 13–17, 34–38

"Night is coming when no one can work. While I am in the world, I am the light of the world" (John 9:4b–5).

REFLECTION: Where last Sunday's reading focused on the baptismal "waters," today's reading focuses on baptismal "light." Everyone knows what is like to stumble around in the dark. You can stub your toe or worse. Anthropologists tell us that the discovery of fire was one of the most important advances of early human beings, not only because it provided the means to cook food but even more primordially, it permitted them to make use of the night. It allowed for freer movement and living in safer environments, like caves.

The contrast between darkness and light is a prominent feature of John's Gospel. Jesus promises that he is the light. John the Baptist already proclaimed this at the beginning of his ministry (John 1:6–9). The story of the man born blind reinforces this assertion.

Jesus allows for true sight. Even a man born blind—that is, blindness not caused by an accident or illness—can be permitted to see when Jesus touches him, anoints him, heals him. The man himself cannot explain the miracle. His parents shirk their own testimony in favor of their son's. Eventually, after rigorous cross-examination, the man comes to "believe"—the all-important response to the presence of Jesus the Messiah (see John 9:38, "I do believe").

The entire sequence serves as a backdrop for the next step toward faith for the catechumens and candidates. At baptism, in addition to the anointing with holy oil, the baptized are also given a small candle reminiscent of the Easter candle that will be lit at the Easter Vigil and throughout the Easter season. This symbolizes that the newly baptized become heralds of the light. They leave the darkness of sin behind and bask in the light of salvation. They become little lights in the darkness.

This transformation, which happens only through God's grace and the gift of the Holy Spirit, is great cause for rejoicing on this Laetare Sunday. The name derives from the first Latin word of the entrance antiphon at Mass (Isa 66:10, "rejoice"). To mark this shift in emphasis on this Sunday, many priests opt to put aside the purple penitential vestments to wear the rose-colored ones, a visual symbol that even in the midst of our penitential season we are aware of the glory of the resurrection. We glimpse the upcoming Easter feast, which will begin with the drama of Holy Saturday night, when the Easter fire will be lit, and the darkened church interiors will slowly come alive with light. Virtually everyone I know who has experienced the Easter Vigil remarks about the impressive visual image of the light overcoming the darkness. It is a universal and dramatic symbol of the power of goodness to defeat evil.

St. Paul picks up on this theme as well, when he reminds the Thessalonians of their baptismal identity: "For all of you are children of the light and children of the day. We are not of the night or of darkness" (1 Thess 5:5).

QUESTION: How has the light of Christ overcome my personal "blindness" to allow me to "see" more clearly what I must be and do?

THE FOURTH SUNDAY, YEAR B

THEME: God So Loved the World

READINGS: 2 Chron 36:14–16, 19–23; Ps 137; Eph 2:4–10; John 3:14–21

"But they mocked God's messengers" (2 Chron 36:16).

REFLECTION: As mentioned in the introduction, there is a shift of tone in the fourth week of Lent, and we see it already in this Sunday's readings. We do not often hear from Second Chronicles, but the reading today tells of the consistent and habitual refusal of God's chosen people to remain obedient to the multiple covenants God offered them. Time and again, the text speaks of Israel's mocking of God's messengers, scoffing at the prophets, and ignoring God's word. The unknown author of Chronicles (called the Chronicler) sees in all this the main reason for the fall of the kingdom of Judah and why the exile in Babylon took place. It was righteous judgment on a stubborn people who regularly refused to abide by the covenant stipulations of God's law. In Lent, we humbly acknowledge this unfortunate history of God's people, and we acknowledge our own participation in it in the circumstances of our own day.

Enter today's gospel reading. Loud and clear, John proclaims perhaps the most famous line in all the Gospels: "For God so loved the world that he gave his only Son" (John 3:16). We see this claim on billboards, on T-shirts and sweatshirts, and on street corners. We might say, without exaggeration, that it is the ultimate response to the sad history of God's people and ourselves regularly following our own path rather than God's. John's reading also explains that those who believe in the Son will not be condemned, but those who fail to believe are *already* condemned (verse 18). It is not really God who condemns us, but our own actions or inactions, our own lack of faith. In the end, faith requires a decision. It cannot be avoided. Do we accept God's generous gift of his Son or not?

This Sunday is not limited to a gloomy review of the history of sin. Far from it. It is also Laetare Sunday, the Sunday of rejoicing (as explained in Year A). Pink vestments replace purple ones. We get a hint that our pilgrimage will not end in failure but in hope, not because of our doing, but because God sent his own Son into the world.

As Jesus's journey to Jerusalem plays out in the remaining two weeks of Lent, we might ask ourselves if we have made the right decision in our lives to follow Christ.

QUESTION: How can I make John 3:16 more than just a catchy line from Scripture?

THE FOURTH SUNDAY, YEAR C

THEME: Undeserved Forgiveness

READINGS: Josh 5:9a, 10–12; Ps 34; 2 Cor 5:17–21; Luke 15:1–3, 11–32

"But now we must celebrate and rejoice, because your brother was dead and has come to life again; he was lost and has been found" (Luke 15:32).

REFLECTION: Have you ever known overindulgent parents? I have. I have seen it numerous times. Children whose parents dote on them, spoil them rotten, only to have these same beneficiaries of excessive love do something terribly offensive and hurtful. When I see it, my blood boils. If I were a parent of such an ungrateful child, I would likely want to punish them somehow—show them who's boss!

The gospel reading for this Sunday (also used on the Saturday of the second week of Lent, above) tells one of the most beloved and memorable stories in the Gospels, usually called the Parable of the Prodigal Son. It is the climactic scene of the entire chapter 15 of Luke, which is devoted exclusively to forgiveness. It concerns two sons and an overly indulgent father. The younger insults his father by asking for his inheritance early (practically insinuating a death wish on him!), only to go out and squander it on unspecified dissolute living. The older son, who stays behind, doing his normal chores and obeying his father, is incensed when the younger son finally reappears on the doorstep. The younger one is only asking to be readmitted as a hired hand, no longer a son. He has come to his senses; he has recognized his guilt.

Then comes the shock. The older son is so upset that his father is seemingly duped into taking this good-for-nothing squanderer back that he refuses to join the party organized to celebrate the prodigal son's return. Even so, the father reaches out to him, too. He pleads that he join the festivity because the lost son has returned. He was virtually dead, but now is back alive. The family can be whole once more.

The real surprise is that the father wants to keep hold of them both. He overlooks the shame of the one and the stinginess of the other. He wants them both. That's the point. God is like that. God operates a kind of lost-and-found department for humanity. God extends undeserved forgiveness to all God's children! Would that we could rejoice in this fact.

Joy is indeed an important aspect at the beginning of this fourth week of Lent. This Sunday marks the approximate midpoint in the Lenten season. As described above in Year A, it is also Laetare Sunday, expressing an attitude of joy that is natural to the Christian message. Undeserved forgiveness brings this joy about. We might say that this Sunday is like a little spiritual oasis in our Lenten desert.

QUESTION: Just how far does my own mercy and love extend, whether in my family or more broadly? Am I able to rejoice when others are forgiven their transgressions?

MONDAY OF THE FOURTH WEEK[1]

THEME: Out with the Old, In with the New

READINGS: Isa 65:17–21; Ps 30; John 4:43–54

"Lo, I am about to create new heavens / and a new earth; The things of the past shall not be remembered / or come to mind" (Isa 65:17).

REFLECTION: It is good that Lent, at least in the northern hemisphere, coincides in large measure with late winter and early spring. Nothing invigorates me more once the weather starts to get milder than to get on with spring cleaning. It feels good to throw open the windows, air out the apartment, organize the clothes closet, and prepare for the change of seasons. Sometimes it feels good to divest oneself of the old and embrace the new. Lent provides us an occasion for spiritual housecleaning. It is a time to jettison old, bad habits and to instill a new way of being, rooted in God's grace.

This is indeed the vision of the Book of Isaiah. Today's first reading speaks of "new heavens" and a "new earth." This is part of the prophet's vision that God desires to completely transform the people of Israel and give them new hope and a new existence. This is a vision picked up as well in the New Testament, for instance in St. Paul's image of "new creation" (Gal 6:15; 2 Cor 5:17), which is a symbol of the new life that comes about by virtue of baptism. It is a life transformed *in* Christ. It comes about when we are willing to discard the "old" person and "put on" the new (Eph 4:22–24). The image also reflects the baptismal imagery of stripping off the old clothes and putting on the new (Gal 3:17; Rom 13:14), something that may well reflect early liturgical baptismal practices when the newly baptized were clothed in white garments. It is also the vision of the Book of Revelation (21:1) about what God will do when the time is right:

---

1. The following readings may be used on any day this week, especially in Years B and C when the gospel of the man born blind is not read on the Fourth Sunday of Lent: Mic 7:7–9 and John 9:1–41.

create a new heavens and a new earth. Essentially, God provides an opportunity to start all over again.

The challenge in this situation, of course, is to have the courage to follow through with this spiritual housecleaning. It is not easy to divest oneself of old habits or to change our ways. We all get into ruts. We follow familiar patterns in our life because, well, they are familiar. We are comfortable in them. Change comes with cost. We have to move out of our comfort zones to embrace a new way of living. If we are willing, then God's grace can lead us to take the first courageous step into this new existence. It essentially began at our baptism, but it needs to be renewed over and over again as our old patterns resist this transformation.

QUESTION: What in my life can be considered part of my "old" way of being that I can put away to make room for a new way of being, living more concretely in accordance with God's will?

TUESDAY OF THE FOURTH WEEK

THEME: What Jesus Wants

READINGS: Ezek 47:1–9, 12; Ps 46; John 5:1–16

"'Do you want to be well?' The sick man answered him, 'Sir, I have no one to put me into the pool when the water is stirred up'" (John 5:6b–7a).

REFLECTION: How should we understand Jesus's question to a man who had been ill for thirty-eight years? The text explicitly says, "When Jesus saw him lying there, and knew that he had been ill for a long time," he then pops the question. The poor man had tried time and again to crawl into the pool at the right moment when the waters stirred. Is Jesus serious? Does he really not know how desperate the man is to be healed? After all, the pool was associated with a legend that an angel would stir up the waters to provide healing to the first person to reach the pool at just that moment.

This remarkable story in John's Gospel takes place at a pool of water in Jerusalem called Bethesda (or variants Bethzatha or Bethsaida), meaning "house of healing." It was located near "the Sheep Gate," which likely served as the entrance gate for the sacrificial animals for the temple, providing a convenient means for the purification rituals necessary for the temple sacrifices. Archaeology has confirmed the design of the "five porticoes" mentioned in the story (John 5:2).

As described in the introduction above, this week portrays the increasing hostility toward Jesus. This story occurs here in Lent because it is part of this scenario. It describes the increasingly tense opposition to Jesus the more his ministry of healing affects the lives of ordinary people positively. Jesus's question is not ironic nor mocking. What Jesus wants is our well-being. The crippled man's response to Jesus's question describes his dilemma. He has no one to help him! Jesus's reaction is simple. He tells the man to rise and walk, instantly healing him. The gesture shows that Jesus understood the man's desire and need and wanted to address it. The opponents of Jesus, however, are incensed because the healing takes place on a Sabbath. Their anger only increases when Jesus explains his close relationship to his heavenly Father, and the fact that he and the Father work together for the good of all. This only provokes more plotting against Jesus, which we will see in the remaining days of Lent that lead up to Holy Week.

QUESTION: What do I truly desire from Jesus? What do I believe Jesus wants from me?

WEDNESDAY OF THE FOURTH WEEK

THEME: No Child Left Behind

READINGS: Isa 49:8–15; Ps 145; John 5:17–30

"Can a mother forget her infant, / be without tenderness for the child of her womb? / Even should she forget, / I will never forget you" (Isa 49:15).

REFLECTION: Although it is a rare occurrence, there are (sadly) stories of women who have been bad mothers. There are a few who have abandoned their own children or abused them in one way or another. Bad parenting does happen. Almost every summer, infants or toddlers are left in hot cars with the windows rolled up while the parent goes shopping.

Such events are (happily) the exception. Even in the animal kingdom, mothers often go to great lengths to save their babies. We see from Isaiah in today's reading that the ancient Israelites were also aware that such occurrences could happen, but God prefers to treat us human beings as a nurturing and loving mother would.

In 2001, an act of Congress established a bipartisan national educational program in the United States titled "No Child Left Behind." Its goal was ostensibly to improve dramatically the performance in public settings where underprivileged children were often either neglected or not encouraged sufficiently to learn and grow. By 2015, the national program was so criticized that a replacement act put the primary responsibility on the shoulders of individual states. The goal was admirable, the results much less so. There are still children left behind.

Fortunately for the human race, God is not a bad parent. Israel sometimes felt abandoned, but the prophet Isaiah indicates that God can never do this. Isaiah expresses utter confidence in God's ability to put our interests at the forefront of concern for all creation. God will not, God cannot, leave anyone behind. For the authors of the New Testament, the proof of God's loving nature was in the gift of his only begotten Son for the salvation of the world (see John 3:16). Today's gospel reading emphasizes some aspects of this gratuitous love. The Father gives life, and so does the Son. The Father does not judge but entrusts judgment to the Son, whose righteous judgment reflects his heavenly Father's will. Jesus explains this in explicit terms: "I cannot do anything on my own; I judge as I hear, and my judgment is just, because I do not seek my own will but the will of the one who sent me" (John 5:30). The prefect harmony between Father and Son in this relationship is a reassurance. In Jesus's ministry, we see his Father's love. The apple does not fall far from the tree. The Son reflects the Father in every way.

QUESTION: Have you ever felt abandoned by friends or family? By God? How were you able to work through this feeling?

THURSDAY OF THE FOURTH WEEK

THEME: What's Moses Got to Do with It?

READINGS: Exod 32:7–14 Ps 106; John 5:31–47

"For if you had believed Moses, you would have believed me, because he wrote about me" (John 5:46).

REFLECTION: How could Moses have written about Jesus? Some twelve hundred years separate the two. Moses existed long before Jesus of Nazareth. Yet there is Jesus in John's Gospel stating outright to his enemies that they would have known him, if only they had believed Moses "because he wrote about me. But if you do not believe his writings, how will you believe my words?" (John 5:46b–47).

It would not be an exaggeration to say that Moses has every-thing to do with Jesus! Why? God chose Moses to lead Israel out of bondage in Egypt, and Moses received the law (Hebrew *torah*, "instruction") directly from God on Mount Sinai. In fact, Moses is so identified with the law that his name serves as a cipher for it. To evoke Moses is to recall God's sacred word enshrined in the law and the prophets, what we Christians consider the Old Testament. And from our perspective, everything in the Old Testament prepared for the New Testament. Moses, a great prophet, along with all the prophets, prepared the way for Christ. The challenge is properly reading the Sacred Scriptures, perceiving their truth and their fulfillment in the person of Jesus Christ.

Lent is one of those liturgical seasons where the back and forth between Old Testament and New Testament is most evident. In today's first reading we see Moses interceding with God once more for his stubborn people. Moses eloquently convinces God to relent on the just punishment for this rebellious people. This hallmark of mercy will be even more evident in Jesus, who will willingly sacrifice himself by the ignominy of the cross for the sake of us sinners. Indeed, the Moses connection will come back again in this regard in the form of the "raising up" that Moses did with the bronze serpent in the desert to heal the people of their snake bites (compare Num 21:9 and John 3:14). Learning to read the Scriptures properly is what allows us to perceive the truth within them. They "testify" to Jesus. They verify the truth of God's word. In a sense, the Scriptures are an unbroken line between Moses and Jesus. Our task is to perceive this connection and comprehend why it gives us all the tools we need to understand the mystery of God's will.

QUESTION: How deep is my understanding of the Sacred Scriptures? Do I take time to let them sink in? Do I see connections between the Old and New Testaments?

FRIDAY OF THE FOURTH WEEK

THEME: The Hour

READINGS: Wis 2:1a, 12–22; Ps 34; John 7:1–2, 10, 25–30

"So they tried to arrest him, but no one laid a hand upon him, because his hour had not yet come" (John 7:30).

REFLECTION: I once overheard a farmer explaining to his young nephews the importance of timing in his work. When they asked how this was so, he patiently explained that a farmer had to discern very carefully when to plant, when to fertilize, and when to harvest. If you are not careful, you can mess up the crops. A good farmer keeps an eye on the weather, the condition of the soil, and so on in order to reap the best from his crop. Timing is crucial.

It seems that something similar happened in Jesus's life, at least according to John's Gospel. John uses the expression of "the hour" for that precise time when Jesus can rightly accept his fate and achieve his Father's will. At this point in Lent, we hear stories like in today's gospel reading wherein Jesus could have been arrested by his enemies, but his "hour" had not yet come. Try as they might, they cannot capture him. It is not they who are in charge of this timing, but Jesus himself. Only when the time is right, will he allow himself to proceed to his fate.

When the early Christians read parts of the Old Testament that speak of innocent righteous individuals beset by evildoers, they naturally thought of Jesus. This is the case with today's first reading from the second chapter of the Book of Wisdom. It describes "the just one" who is surrounded by jealous evildoers who want to trap him. They despise him for claiming God as his Father and for scorning their "transgressions of the law" (Wis 2:12). So, they decide to test him, entrap him, and make him suffer for his self-righteousness. This same scenario is exactly how John's Gospel interprets the story of Jesus, albeit viewed from an ironic point of view. Jesus is indeed the innocent just one, wrongly persecuted by unjust opponents. Yet he controls the hour. He embodies incredible patience. He waits and watches. He determines the right timing, the moment at which he will allow himself to be snared. Why? The psalm response today reveals the reasoning. It proclaims, "The LORD is close to the brokenhearted" and "When the just cry out, the LORD hears them." In Christan thought, this is all part of God's mysterious divine plan to deal with sinful humanity.

QUESTION: What is your response to perceived unjust persecution? How capable are you of trusting that God can indeed help the downcast and brokenhearted?

SATURDAY OF THE FOURTH WEEK

THEME: Division and Decision

READINGS: Jer 11:18–20; Ps 7; John 7:40–53

"So a division occurred in the crowd because of him" (John 7:43).

REFLECTION: I have only served once on a jury. In fact, I was the jury foreman. It was a civil trial of no real consequence (in hindsight), but I remember clearly how divided the twelve of us jurors began. We were evenly divided, some believing the litigant and others believing the defendant. Who to believe? Eventually, the plaintiff was found to have lied about the facts and had brought the civil suit out of jealousy, but only 20/20 hindsight revealed this outcome. In the end, the jury ruled unanimously in favor of the defendant, and the case was resolved.

Would that such divisions could be so readily remedied! In today's gospel reading, we hear of a serious division in the crowds regarding Jesus's identity. Some consider him "the Prophet" (apparently a prophetic figure awaited before the end times) and others "the Christ [= Messiah]." Some wanted to have Jesus arrested, while others, like Nicodemus, who eventually became a follower, preferred to proceed cautiously. They desired to hear more from Jesus and search out more of his background. Thus, the division (Greek *schisma*). In John's Gospel, however, divisions are not the final word. Ultimately, individuals and the crowd itself must make a decision. Either you are for Jesus, or you are against him. Either you favor light, life, and truth, or you prefer darkness, death, and falsehoods. Which will it be? It seems that we are right back at the same question that confronted us at the beginning of Lent: What choice will we make?

I suppose many of us today think that had we lived in the time of Jesus, we would readily have recognized him and been able to make the right choice. But is this so? Would we really have been able to perceive Jesus as the long-awaited Messiah? Would his sacred identity have been so evident to us? I have my doubts. I fear that

71

because of how we perceive the truth of the gospel reading today, we naively think we would have found ourselves on the right side of the great divide in Jesus's day. Hindsight is 20/20, but making decisions cannot always await looking in the rearview mirror.

Today's first reading speaks of the prophet Jeremiah seeing himself "like a trusting lamb led to slaughter" who had not initially perceived the terrible plots against him. Yet God revealed the truth to him and allowed him to see how his enemies were plotting his demise. I suspect that Jesus, too, could perceive the opposition. Unlike Jeremiah, however, Jesus did not pray for his enemies' demise but that they might repent of their devious ways. As we move into the fifth week of this Lenten season, the plot against Jesus will thicken. Then we will need to make a decision: whose side are we really on?

QUESTION: What is your response to divisions that occur in the church and in the world in our day? How can such divisions be overcome?

6

THE FIFTH WEEK
OF LENT

THE FIFTH SUNDAY, YEAR A

THEME: Lazarus and the Gift of Eternal Life

READINGS: Ezek 37:12–14; Ps 130; Rom 8:8–11; John 11:1–45 or [shorter version] 11:3–7, 17, 20–27, 33b–45

"'Lazarus, come out!' The dead man came out, tied hand and foot with burial bands, and his face was wrapped in a cloth" (John 11:44).

REFLECTION: In my conversations with elderly individuals, I have frequently heard about the trials and tribulations of growing old. Granted that some people age more gracefully than others, and that some have more fortunate health situations than others, aging is often not easy. Many elderly complain that growing old is not for the faint of heart!

How did Lazarus feel about being revived by Jesus, I wonder? This is, after all, a story of resuscitation, not resurrection. Jesus brought his friend Lazarus back to *this* life but with the promise of life eternal. Lazarus was going to have to enter the tomb once more in order to experience the life that will never end. He prefigures the resurrection. In fact, all the readings in today's celebration speak of life. Ezekiel's

73

magnificent image of opening the graves of the dead and bringing them back to life was originally the promise of restoring Israel. God could place the Spirit in those dead bones and bring them back to life. This is exactly what Jesus did for Lazarus. He brings him out of the tomb and restores him to his family and friends. For John's Gospel, this is the last and ultimate "sign" that Jesus did prior to the initiation of the plot against him by the Jewish leadership council, the Sanhedrin. There is no greater sign that Jesus can offer than the gift of life, resurrected life. Lazarus embodies this image, this promise.

These readings are obviously used in Year A in the context of the final preparation of the catechumens and candidates to experience the newness of life celebrated at the Easter Vigil. Lazarus is the concrete sign that Jesus came to bring life, and that we might "have it more abundantly" (John 10:10). It is the last of Jesus's "signs" in the Gospel of John before the greatest sign of all, the resurrection.

In our modern culture where human life seems to be viewed cheaply, Jesus's promise of eternal life may startle. "Eternal" is not merely a word meaning length of time. It also denotes a *quality* of life. The life of the Spirit goes beyond our human existence. It transports us to another realm, to another dimension. That is the transformation that we celebrate at Easter.

QUESTION: What do I believe about the resurrection of the dead? How deep is my faith that God can indeed provide eternal life for those who believe in his Son Jesus Christ?

THE FIFTH SUNDAY, YEAR B

THEME: Seeing Jesus

READINGS: Jer 31:31–34; Ps 51; Heb 5:7–9; John 12:20–33

"Sir, we would like to see Jesus" (John 12:21).

REFLECTION: When we read the Gospels and hear the stories about Jesus of Nazareth, we could well pose the question, "Who wouldn't want to see Jesus?" The Gospels indicate that Jesus's reputation as a miracle worker, a prophet, and an inspiring teacher provoked a lot of interest. Even those who may not have thought of following him as a Messiah figure appear intrigued to know more about him.

One of the motifs found in John's Gospel is the mystery of Jesus's identity. Where does he come from? What is he really about? In today's gospel reading, a group of unnamed Greeks, non-Jews, come up to one of the disciples, Philip, probably a Jew with a Greek name, and ask to see Jesus. That little question sets off a chain reaction, from Philip, to other disciples, and finally to Jesus himself. The curious thing is that then the Greeks disappear entirely from the story! Did they ever get to see Jesus? We are not told. Instead, this desire leads to a discourse by Jesus that highlights that his "hour" has come. He is nearing the end, getting close to the conclusion of why he came into the world bringing light to dispel the darkness (John 1:9; 8:12).

On this Fifth Sunday of Lent, the intensity of conflict over Jesus's destiny builds, as his opponents seek to trap and even destroy him. The extended talk of the "hour" in today's gospel reading heightens this theme. Yet the "hour" is not merely one in which Jesus will meet his death and fulfill his mission. It is also the hour of "glory." His heavenly Father will be glorified by Jesus's fulfillment of his destiny.

John's Gospel also presents the beautiful image of the grain of wheat that must fall to the ground to die in order to bear much fruit. It is a metaphor for Jesus's own sacrifice. It also offers us an appropriate lesson as we prepare to follow Jesus intensely in his final days. Following him means taking up our own cross. It means learning to make sacrifices that can bear unexpected fruit.

QUESTION: What "fruit" do I bear in my life that gives evidence that I have truly followed Jesus?

THE FIFTH SUNDAY, YEAR C

THEME: Something New

READINGS: Isa 43:16–21; Ps 126; Phil 3:8–14; John 8:1–11

"Neither do I condemn you. Go, [and] from now on do not sin anymore" (John 8:15).

REFLECTION: Like most people, I like to get something new once in a while. Although I am not into conspicuous consumption and don't even particularly like shopping, occasionally getting something new feels good. After seventeen years, I finally bought a new car, a hybrid. What a different experience to have that "new car smell" for some months, and to get great gas mileage! But what if the "something new" was not an object but something intangible yet infinitely more important? Like not being judged even when we are guilty!

The first reading for this Fifth Sunday of Lent comes from the prophet Isaiah. The prophet describes the Lord's bringing the desert back to life, a symbol of hope for a people too long in exile. Isaiah exclaims, "See, I am doing something new!" (43:19). The totally unexpected rebirth in the desert is actually coming to fruition. God has the ability to restore the people from exile and to revive their hope in a totally unexpected way. That is the way God's grace works. It surprises. Today's gospel reading provides even a more remarkable image along the same lines, but first we need to recall some facts about John's Gospel.

This story of the woman caught in adultery—as it is usually and unfortunately titled—has a curious history. Even though it is found at the beginning of chapter 8 in John's Gospel, the story is actually missing from all the early Greek manuscripts of this Gospel. It seems to be a misplaced story. It's language and theological outlook are more at home in Luke's Gospel than in John's. Yet here it is. The setting is before the temple in Jerusalem, and some of Jesus's opponents bring the woman (only!) blatantly caught in the act of adultery to test him (Where's the guilty man? Lev 20:10 prescribes judgment for both parties.). They want to see if he will apply the law of Moses literally, which required death for adulterers. Surprisingly, Jesus does not give an answer. Instead, he bends down and begins to write on the ground with his finger (John 8:6). What was he writing? The text does not say. What happens, though, is telling. One by one the accusers, "beginning with the elders," slip away. Was Jesus writing out *their* sins? Was he just doodling? Drawing a picture? The text is silent. Whatever it was, only Jesus and the woman are left in front of one another. Then, when she admits that no one has condemned her, Jesus springs the surprise: "Neither do I condemn you."

This is indeed something new and unexpected. It is divine mercy in action. It is gratuitous and undeserved, but it does come with a proviso: go and sin no more. Surely, this is not asking too much for one who has received so generously. Grace begets grace. It leads to transformation.

QUESTION: How readily am I willing to condemn rather than be merciful? Have I received mercy gratefully?

MONDAY OF THE FIFTH WEEK[1]

THEME: The Testimony of the Light

READINGS: Dan 13:1–9, 15–17, 19–30, 33–62 or 13:41c–62; Ps 23; John 8:12–20 (second choice, if John 8:1–11 is read on the previous Sunday)

"Even in your law it is written that testimony of two men can be verified" (John 8:17).

REFLECTION: In the Jewish law it was a standard practice to accept the testimony of two witnesses with regard to accusations of

---

1. The following readings may be used on any day this week, especially in Years B and C when the gospel of Lazarus is not read on the Fifth Sunday of Lent: 2 Kgs 4:18b–21, 32–37; John 11:1–45.

a crime (see Deut 17:6 and 19:15). Jesus refers to this teaching in his controversy with some of his Jewish opponents in today's gospel reading. In the patriarchally oriented society of ancient Israel, this generally meant "men," though the translation is faulty in this instance, since the Greek word (*anthrōpos*) means "human beings," not "men." The reality, though, was that women generally were not deemed reliable witnesses (see Luke 24:11, where the women's testimony is not believed). We see this reflected in the first reading from the Book of Daniel. A young woman is falsely accused by two lecherous old men who tried in vain to seduce her. They falsely accuse her of having relations with an elusive (and nonexistent) young suitor. Enter the young prophet Daniel. Wiser than his age would indicate, he separates the two old men and discovers their treachery. Their own words condemn them, as each one names a different kind of tree under which the alleged seduction took place. Daniel's perceptive grilling of the two false witnesses reveals their deception and sheds light on the truth. Fortunately, the young woman is saved from an ignominious death because of his righteous action.

This first reading is rightly paired with today's gospel reading. In response to Jesus's declaration that he is "the light of the world," his opponents accuse him of testifying on his own behalf, and thus not having an adequate number of witnesses. What we see at the beginning of this fifth week of Lent is an intensified opposition to Jesus. His opponents fail time and again to trap him because they are myopic. They do not know that Jesus's heavenly Father provides all the testimony needed. Jesus is truly the light of the world, but his opponents consistently prefer darkness. Unlike the woman in the first reading, Jesus only temporarily escapes death, for "his hour had not yet come" (John 11:20).

QUESTION: The eighth commandment prohibits bearing false witness against someone (Exod 20:16; Deut 5:20). Yet how often is it violated? Why do people bear false witness? What can inhibit it?

TUESDAY OF THE FIFTH WEEK

THEME: Lift High the Cross

READINGS: Num 21:4–9; Ps 102; John 8:21–30

"When you lift up the Son of Man, then you will come to realize that I AM" (John 8:28).

REFLECTION: Readers may have heard of a phenomenon that often happens when young women and men head off to college. It is called "the freshmen fifteen." Apparently, when young people leave home and go to higher education, they discover that cafeteria food is not nearly as attractive as mom and dad's home-cooked fare. Either they increase their intake with whatever appeals to them, or they take refuge in fast food and frequent snacks. The resulting weight gain is usually noticeable! I myself remember times when the institutional food that I had to endure was indeed unappealing. I could identify with the complaint of the Israelites against Moses in today's first reading: "Why have you brought us up from Egypt to die in the wilderness, where there is no food or water? We are disgusted with this wretched food!" (Num 21:5).

The context of today's first reading is, of course, the experience of the Israelites while wandering in the desert after their escape from slavery in Egypt. Suddenly freedom seems less attractive than they thought. They have to endure bad food and water! So, they grumble against God and his spokesman, Moses. It is not the food complaint, however, that is the focus of this reading, paired as it is with today's gospel reading; rather, it concerns the punishment that God sends upon the Israelites for their insolence and its aftermath. God sends serpents who bite and kill the complainers. Only after Moses's intervention on their behalf does God relent. He tells Moses to place a bronze serpent on a pole. Those bitten by the serpents need only to look upon the image to be healed. This provides the focus for our attention.

The same image is picked up in today's gospel reading. John's Gospel associates the "lifting up" of the Son of Man with the saving action of God in the desert. Instead of a bronze serpent, it is Jesus who is lifted up on a cross who brings about salvation. Once more the Gospel associates the divine name "I AM" with Jesus. His true identity is intimately tied to his Father. Everything Jesus does reflects his Father's will: "I say only what the Father taught me" (John 8:28b). Jesus does only what the Father has asked of him. Being lifted high on the cross is intended to draw us toward him, who is the face of the Father's mercy. We may well still complain about one situation or another that makes us suffer, but gazing upon the Crucified One reveals the Father's true love for all humanity.

QUESTION: What does the cross or crucifix mean to me? Do my actions as a Christian bear witness to the cross of Christ?

WEDNESDAY OF THE FIFTH WEEK

THEME: Slavery…to What?

READINGS: Dan 3:14–20, 91–92, 95; responsorial: Dan 3:52–56; John 8:31–42

"A slave does not remain in a household forever, but a son always remains" (John 8:35).

REFLECTION: In the twenty-first century we know well that literal slavery—making or seeing fellow human beings as chattels or property—is morally wrong and utterly reprehensible. Although there are sadly still instances of true human slavery in our day, most cultures prohibit it and work against it. But "slavery" can also have another meaning beyond the literal. Today's readings show us how slavery can be metaphorically a reality even today. Consider, for instance, addictions. They are a kind of slavery. Addictions to alcohol, drugs, tobacco, sex, gambling, and social media, for example, continue to enslave people. Even addiction to work (workaholism) or to incessantly buying things (consumerism) might be considered a type of slavery. Today's readings speak to us of slavery to sin, something all human beings suffer, even if we may not always acknowledge it. Lent is a season in which we try to master this human proclivity and not let it dominate us.

The gospel reading today continues the controversy between Jesus and some of his interlocutors. In this instance, they are fellow "Jews who believed in him." Their problem is that they still do not recognize Jesus for who he is: the true Son of his heavenly Father. They themselves tout their being descendants of Abraham, and Jesus affirms this. What Jesus does not affirm, however, is that their deeds reflect this Abrahamic identity. If they were true "sons [and daughters]" of Abraham, they would act like it. They would act according to the covenant with God. And they would recognize Jesus as the Father's true Son. This is what leads Jesus to contrast the existence of a slave with that of a son or daughter who remains always a member of the family.

The first reading relates to this controversy, albeit from a different perspective. The three faithful young Israelites, Shadrach, Meshach, and Abednego, show themselves to be entirely free individuals. They refuse to succumb to King Nebuchadnezzar's insistence that they worship a golden statue. In other words, they are being tempted to violate God's prohibition against idols (Exod 2:3–4; Lev 26:1) and enslave themselves to idolatry. Even the threat of being thrown into a fiery furnace does not dissuade them. So, Nebuchadnezzar tosses them in, only to see them survive it, alongside another who "looks like a son of God." The king is reduced to having to acclaim the three who refused his command and "yielded their bodies rather than serve or worship any god except their own God." That is the price of remaining a true son and not merely a slave. Their sacrifice foreshadows that of Jesus. As Lent proceeds and Holy Week looms, our focus is on Jesus who shows himself always to be the faithful Son of God, suffering Son of Man, and Savior of the world whom we have come to know. In his Sonship, we have our own identity. In his sacrifice we find our salvation.

QUESTION: In what ways am I "enslaved"? What can I do to live more freely in accordance with God's will?

THURSDAY OF THE FIFTH WEEK

THEME: A Host of Nations

READINGS: Gen 17:3–9; Ps 105; John 8:51–59

"My covenant with you is this: you are to become the father of a host of nations" (Gen 17:4).

REFLECTION: Abraham is considered to be the father of the faith of three of the world's main religions: Judaism, Christianity, and Islam. How is it that one such ancient figure could be the source of three distinct religions, which unfortunately have not had a history of getting along with one another? The key is in the notion of *covenant.*

In our modern western society, we have seen the erosion of the ability of human beings to adhere to agreements. We pay lip service to the notion of covenants in multiple ways, such as marriages, legal contracts, and even our "vocation." Yet we struggle to make such agreements endure. Even where loyalty is expressed as a value to be upheld—for example, companies with their employees—the value is often only symbolic. Just think of the divorce rate, or of the inability of many modern people to make a firm and lasting life commitment. Covenants have become rather temporary. So long as the terms are convenient, then the covenant sticks. If circumstances change, then the covenant changes too.

This is not the case with God. The psalm response today announces: "The LORD remembers his covenant forever" (Ps 105:8). This is exactly what God promised Abraham, as narrated in the first reading. God promised innumerable progeny, a land, and a "host of nations." Abraham was to be the father who joined all peoples together and who welcomed people from distant lands. This was God's promise. For his part, Abraham was to keep God's commands, even if they were sometimes baffling, such as the puzzling order to sacrifice his own son Isaac (Genesis 22), which nonetheless is seen as a forerunner of the sacrifice of Jesus.

Jesus knew of the importance of Abraham. He makes this clear in today's gospel reading. In the midst of a controversy with his Jewish opponents, who (rightly) claim Abraham as their ancestor, Jesus mysteriously asserts that "Before Abraham came to be, I AM" (John 8:59). The strange expression "I AM" is, of course, the divine name revealed to Moses in the burning bush (Exod 3:14). In essence, Jesus properly employs the divine name, equating himself with God his heavenly Father and thus incensing his opponents.

QUESTION: How deeply do you believe in the universality of the faith, that God desires that *all* humanity, *all* nations, *all* peoples, embrace the extraordinary offer of covenantal love?

FRIDAY OF THE FIFTH WEEK

THEME: The Suffering Prophet

READINGS: Jer 20:10–13; Ps 18; John 10:31–42

"But the LORD is with me, like a mighty champion: / my persecutors will stumble, they will not triumph" (Jer 20:11).

REFLECTION: One of the first cases in pastoral counseling that I had to deal with as a young priest was a young woman who quite evidently was paranoid. She was convinced that *everyone* was against her. *Everyone* was out to get her. Her family, her work colleagues, even some of her perceived friends, according to her estimation, were against her. She came to me for some help, but I quickly recognized that her problems were far beyond my capabilities in pastoral counseling. She needed real psychiatric help, which eventually she received. While I never knew what ultimately happened to her, I have never forgotten the helplessness that was so apparent in her situation when she boiled everything down to a conspiracy against her.

Today's combined readings pair the prophet Jeremiah and Jesus. Neither was paranoid. They had very real enemies. The seventh-century-BCE prophet Jeremiah is the quintessential suffering prophet of the Old Testament. He was indeed persecuted. Later Jewish tradition claims that his fellow Jews took him into Egypt because they despised his prophetic message. There allegedly he was martyred. No wonder Jeremiah in today's first reading claims, "I hear the whisperings of many: / 'Terror on every side! / Denounce! / Let us denounce him!'" The psalm response expresses Jeremiah's confidence in God to protect him: "In my distress I called upon the LORD, and he heard my voice." Yet in his own words, Jeremiah expresses an unsettling attitude. He prays to God against his enemies: "Let me witness the vengeance you take on them."

In today's gospel reading, Jesus is in an even more dire situation. Some fellow Jews pick up rocks to stone him, allegedly for "blasphemy" in identifying himself with God. Jesus escapes their grasp at this point in the story, for his "hour" has not yet arrived. But Jesus's response to this severe opposition is not to call down vengeance upon them but to point to his *deeds*. If his enemies do not like his words, could they not at least look at his actions and perceive that he indeed is doing the Father's good will? Of course, we know that when people have made up their minds, no amount of counterargument will work to persuade them otherwise. True prophets, in particular, have always been victims from this perspective.

As Lent progresses to its inevitable conclusion in Holy Week, we perceive the story of Jesus in all its irony. He was truly God's Son, the Light of the world, the bearer of truth. Yet he also voluntarily accepted his prophetic destiny. No vengeance here. Only humble submission for the sake of saving a world that has trouble accepting the truth of the gospel.

QUESTION: Who are the suffering prophets of our day?

SATURDAY OF THE FIFTH WEEK

THEME: One for the Many

READINGS: Ezek 37:21–28; responsorial: Jer 31:10–13; John 11:45–56

"It is better for you that one man should die instead of the people, so that the whole nation may not perish" (John 11:50).

REFLECTION: We are all familiar with inspiring tales of heroes who sacrifice themselves for the sake of a family, a tribe, or a people. Movies and novels provide a host of such heroic figures. Yet the statement from today's gospel reading cited above is not simply about an ordinary "hero." These words are spoken by the high priest Caiaphas, who ironically speaks the truth about Jesus's fate while thinking it to be the solution to getting rid of a troublemaking prophet whom some Jews thought to be the Messiah. The author of the Gospel goes on to explain the truth of Caiaphas' words: "He prophesied that Jesus was going to die for the nation and not only for the nation, but also to gather into one the dispersed children of God" (John 11:52). On the eve of Holy Week, this judgment sets in motion the plot to kill Jesus.

If an individual makes a decision to sacrifice himself or herself for the sake of others, we would likely count that as heroic. But if someone else makes the decision to sacrifice another individual's life for the sake of a community, would we evaluate this judgment the same way? I doubt it. It would be tantamount to murder, even if for a "good cause." This is why Caiaphas's words are ironic. They speak a truth beyond what he realizes. Jesus is actually the good shepherd who *voluntarily* lays down his life for his sheep (John 10:17). No one takes his life from him (John 10:18). Jesus freely offers himself for the sake not only of his people but the whole world. This is part of God's plan for a world sorely in need of salvation. The prophet Ezekiel had also foreseen the way God's graciousness works, as evident in today's first reading. Ezekiel recounts God's promise to restore the people into one nation. No longer would it be split in two, as had happened when the northern kingdom of Israel and the southern kingdom of Judah were torn asunder after the death of King Solomon (tenth century BCE).

What kind of love allows for this type of voluntary sacrifice? It is a love beyond our capacity to comprehend. It is a love that knows no bounds. One is sacrificed for many, in fact, for all.

QUESTION: There are countless stories of heroism in which an individual was sacrificed for the sake of a larger reality. How can I respond to this great act of cosmic love seen in Jesus's sacrifice?

7

HOLY WEEK AND THE TRIDUUM

PALM SUNDAY OF THE PASSION OF THE LORD, YEAR A

READINGS: For the blessing of palms—Matt 21:1–11; for Mass: Isa 50:4–7; Ps 22; Phil 2:6–11; Matt 26:14—27:66

"My God, My God, why have you forsaken me?" (Matt 27:46).

REFLECTION: Palm Sunday has its own inherent theme each year in Lent. It concerns the passion of Jesus. The recollection of the entry into Jerusalem is but a prelude. The same readings are proclaimed that commemorate Jesus's joyous entrance into Jerusalem, the city of his fate. Each of the three years, though, utilizes the individual narratives of the Synoptic Gospel of the year. So, this year it is Matthew's version of the entrance into Jerusalem and also his version of the passion narrative. Since the readings are so rich in meaning, it is impossible to briefly summarize them in an efficient manner. I will only provide a few highlights that might lead you to reflect profitably on each Sunday's unique emphases.

In addition to the passion narrative, each Palm Sunday uniformly uses other readings, including the third of the Suffering Servant

Songs from Isaiah, Psalm 22, which contains some allusions appropriate to the passion of Jesus, and the magnificent Pauline hymn from the Letter to the Philippians. Each of these contributes to the overall understanding that what happened to Jesus was not only a fulfillment of the Old Testament prophecies but also a tremendous humbling of himself in order to be exalted by his heavenly Father. Each reading separately warrants some meditation time on its own. But combined, they provide an even more moving reflection on why Holy Week is so important. Not only do Jesus's enemies make progress in their opposition to him, but his own disciples get into the act. Judas betrays, Peter denies, and all of them desert Jesus, except for some women who had followed him throughout his ministry.

For today's gospel reading, let me point out just a few salient points that are special to Matthew's version of these events:

- Instead of one animal for Jesus to ride into Jerusalem, Matthew speaks of two, an ass and a colt, perhaps reflecting his tendency to double images, as he does elsewhere in his Gospel.
- While waving their palm fronds in the air, the crowds shout homage to Jesus as the "son of David," a title Matthew associates with Jesus's healing ministry.
- Matthew records the excitement and enthusiasm of the crowds welcoming Jesus as their "king," using the unusual word "quaking" (in Greek, *seiō*), tying into the cosmic nature of the events in Jesus's life (also 2:2; 27:51, 54).
- Matthew's Gospel includes the unique story of the tragic fate of Judas, the betrayer (27:3–10).
- Peter's Galilean accent, which apparently gives him away at his denial of Jesus, is mentioned (27:73).
- Jesus appears before Pontius Pilate the "governor" (27:2), reminiscent of his prediction that his followers would also have to appear before governors (10:18).

- At the cross the centurion "and those with him" (27:54) confess Jesus as the Son of God, symbolizing the welcome of the Gentiles into the faith.
- Matthew includes the legend that the disciples had stolen Jesus's body after its burial (27:62–66).

QUESTION: The passion story is truly a "way of the cross." How can I more fully enter into this part of my pilgrimage during this holiest week of the liturgical year?

PALM SUNDAY OF THE PASSION OF THE LORD, YEAR B

READINGS: For the blessing of palms—Mark 11:1–10 or John 12:12–16; for Mass: Isa 50:4–7; Ps 22; Phil 2:6–11; Mark 14:1—15:47

"Truly this man was the Son of God!" (Mark 15:39).

REFLECTION: As was mentioned in the Year A readings for this Sunday, each version of Palm Sunday depends on the individual gospel story of the day. Granted that the basic passion story is the same in its primary outline, small details in the narrative indicate the individual evangelist's interests. Nevertheless, this day's liturgy always begins with the blessing of palms and the reenactment of Jesus's solemn entrance into Jerusalem. Perhaps something we should remember on this occasion is the fickleness of the crowds. When Jesus first arrives, they shout out Hosannas and are ecstatic at his coming. They cry out, "Blessed is he who comes in the name of the Lord!" (Mark 11:9–10). Yet it is not many days later that these shouts of joy will be transformed into shouts of "Crucify him!" (Mark 15:13–14). Crowds can be like that. One minute you're their hero, the next you're their enemy. Yet we must always remember that for Jesus, the passion is but the fulfillment of the Scriptures and his Father's will (Mark 14:49).

Today, Mark's version provides the focus. Allow me to point out a few essential details:

- At the arrest of Jesus, only Mark mentions the "young man" who ran off naked, leaving his linen cloth (in Greek, *sindōn*) behind (14:51–52); the same Greek word is used for the burial cloth for Jesus.
- When Jesus is mocked by the soldiers in the governor's headquarters, they clothe him with a royal "purple" cloak (15:17) not a soldier's scarlet cloak (as in Matthew). This ties into Mark's theme of Jesus as a true "king."
- Simon of Cyrene, who helped Jesus bear the crossbeam and was "the father of Alexander and Rufus" (15:21) is mentioned, perhaps indicating men known in the community.
- Both bandits crucified with Jesus mock him from their own crosses (15:32), unlike in Luke, where one defends Jesus.
- At the cross, the centurion who confesses Jesus as "truly the Son of God" (15:39) is the only *human* character in the story to confess Jesus thus; previously, only demons had professed him as such. The centurion, a non-Jew, is thus ironically the only one to perceive the truth about Jesus.
- Reflecting early Christian memory, Mark records that Mary Magdalene and Mary the mother of Joses were at the crucifixion and saw where Jesus was buried (15:47), which is why they know where to go early on Easter morning to anoint Jesus's body (16:1).

QUESTION: In the story of Jesus's passion, where would I have found myself? As a disciple afraid to defend my master? As a soldier or enemy of Jesus ready to crucify him? As one of the women who stayed and watched the whole affair?

PALM SUNDAY OF THE PASSION OF THE LORD, YEAR C

READINGS: For the blessing of palms—Luke 19:28–40; for Mass: Isa 50:4–7; Ps 22; Phil 2:6–11; Luke 22:14—23:56 or [shorter version] 23:1–49

"Father, into your hands I commend my spirit" (Luke 23:46).

REFLECTION: One of the greatest challenges for those who try seriously to enter into the "spirituality" of this holiest week of the liturgical year is to avoid harmonizing the four gospel stories of the passion of Jesus. This is a natural tendency, of course, and an ancient one. But it is to be resisted. Why? To try to get the flavor of each unique version of what we know was Jesus's fate in the final week of his earthly life. There are four portraits of Jesus of Nazareth (the four Gospels), but there is only *one* Jesus Christ. Each evangelist tells the story in his own way, most likely because it served the needs of their individual communities. While many of the details are the same, the nuances are worth perceiving.

Let's take Luke's version of the entrance into Jerusalem, for instance. It begins the liturgy on this sacred day. For Luke, this solemn entrance into the holy city is the culmination of Jesus's long journey that had begun at 9:51, where the text says, "When the days for his ascension were fulfilled, he set his face to journey to Jerusalem" (my translation). Unlike the other versions, Luke's language reveals that this is a prophetic action on Jesus's part and that it will lead to his passion, death, and resurrection ("ascension"; in Greek, *analēmpseōs*). Jesus's long journey is thus achieved when he arrives and is greeted by the crowds waving palms and crying out in joy. Luke's wording of the singing is also unique, for it harks back to the birth of Jesus. The crowds' words echo the song of the angels at the Nativity: "Peace in heaven / and glory in the highest!" (compare Luke 19:38 and 2:14). Jesus's birth heralds his sacrificial death. Both bring peace and joy.

Luke's passion story also has many unique elements. Below are just a few:

- When Peter denies Jesus in fulfillment of Jesus's prediction at the Last Supper, Luke says that "the Lord turned and looked at Peter" (22:61), sparking Peter's remembrance of the prophecy, and asserting their proximity to one another in this dramatic moment.
- When Pilate learns that Jesus is a Galilean, he sends him to (King) Herod Antipas who happens to be in Jerusalem at the time and desires to see Jesus; finding no guilt, Herod sends Jesus back to Pilate, and the two previous enemies become friends thereafter (23:6–16).
- Multiple declarations of Jesus's innocence are made by different individuals (23:4, 14, 22, 41).
- Jesus looks down on those crucifying him and says, "Father, forgive them, they know not what they do" (23:34; though not all ancient manuscripts have this verse).
- One of the two criminals crucified with Jesus taunts him to save them, while the second admits Jesus's innocence and asks to be remembered in his kingdom, to which Jesus promises that he will be with him "in Paradise" that very day (23:43).
- At his last breath, Jesus prayerfully offers his spirit to his Father in heaven with the line quoted above (23:46).

The result of such small details is to sharpen the portrait of Jesus as an innocent victim who nevertheless continues his public ministry of bringing reconciliation and forgiveness even in the most difficult moments of his own suffering. Thus, Luke's portrait reinforces Jesus's words at the Last Supper about the "new covenant in my blood, which will be shed for you" (22:20).

Naturally, the first reading from one of the Suffering Servant Songs, and the second from Paul's hymn about Christ as the one who voluntarily accepted death on a cross, support the entire presentation of the Lord's passion. The best recommendation to appreciate this pairing is to simply sit with the readings and let them speak to your heart.

QUESTION: If we are honest with ourselves, with which of the two criminals crucified with Jesus would we identify? Would we really recognize Jesus's innocence? Would we want only to save ourselves?

MONDAY OF HOLY WEEK

THEME: The Anointed Servant

READINGS: Isa 42:1–7; Ps 27; John 12:1–11

"Here is my servant whom I uphold, / my chosen one with whom I am pleased" (Isa 42:1).

REFLECTION: In my more reflective moments, I have often wondered what it would have been like to know Jesus of Nazareth in the flesh. The huge success of the popular television series of gospel vignettes called *The Chosen* (2017 to the present) strikes me as an indication that I am not alone. The creators of this innovative retelling of the gospel stories clearly try to get at the human drama behind the scenes, as well as being as faithful as possible to the literal text of the Gospels. Yes, the creators took some artistic license in telling the "backstories" of the characters, but there is a tone of verisimilitude in the portrayal. There is no attempt to whitewash the gospel narratives, nor is there an overly rationalistic answer to what are clearly mysterious circumstances, for instance, in some of the miracle stories.

My question to myself is: Would I have been able to recognize Jesus as the Messiah? Would I have been able to perceive his identity?

The early Christians clearly read the only Scriptures that they knew—what we call the Old Testament—with a view to seeking guidance about explaining how and why Jesus of Nazareth was actually the Son of God and Savior of the world. They sought out, and found, certain echoes that rang true in the story of Jesus. This week is a prime example. On Monday, Tuesday, Wednesday, and Good Friday, the first reading each day is one of the four Suffering Servant Songs (or Hymns) found in the Book of Isaiah the prophet. When the early Christians read these poetic passages (or more accurately heard them proclaimed orally), their minds connected them with Jesus. He was the embodiment of this "suffering servant." Historically speaking, it is uncertain whom the prophet was trying to identify in his own context. Scholars surmise that the anonymous suffering servant is intended to be Israel herself, as a renewed people after having suffered so often in history. The gospel writers do not associate these four hymns only with the passion of Jesus. Matthew, for example, cites part of today's text (Isa 42:1, along with Ps 2:7) at the baptism of Jesus (Matt 3:17), thus affirming Jesus's identity as God's beloved Son. Coupled with today's gospel reading of Mary's anointing of Jesus in preparation for his death reinforces Jesus's identity as the anointed servant of the Lord. He is the one who will accept the suffering that comes his way because of this sacred identity. He will not turn away from it.

As this holiest of all weeks begins, we turn our gaze once more toward the cross and its ultimate message of hope. Jesus fulfilled what the Old Testament had promised. He incarnated in his suffering and death what was needed for the salvation of the world.

QUESTION: How readily do I see in Jesus's suffering a model for the trials and tribulations of my own life? What can I learn from Jesus about the role of suffering in this life?

TUESDAY OF HOLY WEEK

THEME: The Darkness Will Not Overcome

READINGS: Isa 49:1–6; Ps 71; John 13:21–33, 36–38

"Master, where are you going?" (John 13:36).

REFLECTION: Everyone knows the power of darkness. Sometimes it hides illegal or immoral activities. At other times, darkness is simply the absence of light, such as when the electricity goes off at night during a violent storm. In any case, we all know that darkness is often unpleasant.

The Bible makes wide use of the contrast between light and darkness. There is something innately human about these opposites that make them attractive. Often they provide a moral contrast, as in the Letters of Paul (Rom 13:12; 1 Cor 4:5; 1 Thess 5:5). At other times they are more symbolic. Today's gospel reading evokes darkness just as Judas the betrayer accepts the morsel of bread from Jesus while reclining at table at the Last Supper. The text from John dramatically and simply announces: "And it was night" (13:30). Judas's betrayal is an activity of the night. Judas has become an instrument of the darkness.

Today's first reading also mentions light. This excerpt from Isaiah constitutes the second of the four Suffering Servant Songs. Note, however, that it does not simply focus on the suffering aspect of the Servant's duty. In this instance, God pronounces a profound duty: "I will make you *a light to the nations,* / that my salvation may reach to the ends of the earth" (Isa 49:6, emphasis added). This universal light stands in stark contrast to Judas's dark night of betrayal. The Servant—incarnated in Jesus who will soon undergo his passion and death on a cross—serves a larger purpose. His action will be the salvation of the whole world. His will be a universal and inclusive act of love. Jesus knows this. He speaks of it as a moment of glorification. He also sees it as the moment when he will have to go away, to return to the Father. This was always his destiny. He had descended from above so that he could re-ascend to the Father; he was the light come into the world so that people would not live in darkness (John 1:1–14). Yet this is where the misunderstanding of his disciples comes to the fore. Simon Peter speaks once more for the others, asking, "Master, where are you going?" In John, such questions appear regularly on the lips of the disciples because they do not fully comprehend what Jesus is about, where he is from, and where he is going.

In this last week of Lent, the mystery that is such a strong element in the Gospel of John begins to culminate in the passion narrative. All has prepared for Jesus's final "hour," the time when his true purpose for coming into the world would be achieved. For us who relive these sacred moments, we are given an occasion to dwell on the mystery. Take some time to let it all sink in.

QUESTION: What aspects of my life give off "light" to others, and which ones perhaps reflect "darkness"?

WEDNESDAY OF HOLY WEEK

THEME: Spy Wednesday

READINGS: Isa 50:4–9a; Ps 69; Matt 26:14–25

"They paid him thirty pieces of silver" (Matt 26:13).

REFLECTION: When I was a boy, I remember this day being called "Spy Wednesday." I do not know how widespread this custom was among Catholics, but the reason for the label was self-evident. The gospel reading of the day is centered on the betrayal of Jesus by one of his own twelve apostles, Judas Iscariot. His name features among the famous traitors of history, like Ephialtes of Trachis (who betrayed the Spartans in 480 BCE), Marcus Junius Brutus the Younger (who betrayed Julius Caesar in 44 BCE), Guy Fawkes (who tried to blow up the British Parliament in 1605), or Benedict Arnold (who betrayed America in 1780). You get the idea. Some names are automatically tied to betrayal.

In the case of Judas, some details tied to this day are worthy of reflection. Matthew explains that Judas approached the chief priests who opposed Jesus to inquire about how much they would pay him if he betrayed his master. He initiates the betrayal. The precise motivation is not clear. Some traditions surrounding Judas hint that he was greedy, and thus sought money and even used to steal from the common purse of the apostles used to support the poor (see John 12:6), but the agreed upon price of thirty pieces of silver—despite its high-sounding tone—is not a great sum of money. It was the price paid to the owner of a slave who had been gored by an ox (Exod 21:32). Even more important, though, is the symbolic meaning of the sum given by the prophet Zechariah. After shepherding some merchants' flock, the prophet approached the flock's owners and asked to be paid, if they thought his work had been worthy. They counted out the sum of thirty pieces of silver, a haughty and stingy gesture, indicating that they did not much like the prophet's shepherding (Zech 11:12). In response, Zechariah, with biting irony ("the handsome price"), took the same money and flung it into "the treasury in the house of the LORD" (Zech 11:13). This is the same gesture of Judas described in today's gospel reading, but then Judas despairs for having done his treachery. According to a tradition unique to Matthew's Gospel, Judas went out and hanged himself (Matt 27:3–10). The same passage explains that the Jewish leaders did not want to hold onto the money, as it was blood money used for the death of an "innocent" man (Matt 27:6). So, they used it to purchase a potter's field to bury the poor (Matt 27:10).

Betrayal and treason are nasty concepts, to be sure. Most curious is that Christian memory would not have tried to hide this unflattering image of a handpicked disciple of Jesus. Even more telling is that in Matthew's list of the twelve apostles, Simon Peter is listed first and Judas Iscariot, with the descriptor "betrayer," is listed last (Matt 10:1–4). The rest are in between, yet not one of them remained behind when Jesus was arrested in the garden of Gethsemane (Matt 26:56).

Spy Wednesday is a good day to reflect on the ease with which, despite the best of intentions, even the most devoted followers of Jesus could fall apart at the crucial moment. Each of us has within us the capacity to dissemble in the face of danger or adversity, despite our heartfelt protestations. Perhaps we can simply admit, "there but for the grace of God go I."

QUESTION: Have I ever experienced betrayal? Have I ever betrayed anyone? How can you transcend how this experience may have made you feel?

The Triduum

HOLY THURSDAY

Chrism Mass

READINGS: Isa 61:1–3a, 6a, 8b–9; Ps 89; Rev 1:5–8;
Luke 4:16–21

REFLECTION: The instruction in the Roman Missal indicates
that the Chrism Mass may be celebrated on a suitable day before
Holy Thursday. In fact, in the past—and still at the Vatican in
Rome—the Chrism Mass was always celebrated on the morning of
Holy Thursday. This special Mass is particularly important for the
priests of a diocese, as it is the solemn occasion to concelebrate with
the local ordinary (bishop) and to reinforce the bonds of the priest-
hood. During the Mass, the priests renew their priestly promises,
and the people announce their prayerful support for their priests.
Deacons, also, are highlighted in this Mass, since they usually carry
the sacred oils to be blessed by the bishop.

Since this Mass, and all the ceremonies of the Triduum, have
their own special focus, I will not provide a separate theme for each.
The readings are assembled according to an inherent theme appropriate to the day or ceremony. That will suffice.

One other special feature of the Chrism Mass is that it is the
occasion of the blessing of the holy oils that are used throughout
the year. These are the Oil of the Sick, the Oil of the Catechumens,
and the Sacred Chrism itself. Each of these holy oils is used for special occasions, and they are distributed throughout the parishes and
institutions of a diocese. In many dioceses, catechumens and candidates who will be baptized or accepted into the Catholic faith at the
Easter Vigil attend the Chrism Mass. Often an impressive ceremony,

it illustrates the universality of the Catholic faith. If you have never attended a Chrism Mass, I encourage you to do so. These days, this Mass is often held on a different day of the week, or even a few days before Holy Week, in order to permit a wider participation of the clergy to show their solidarity with the bishop.

Evening Mass of the Lord's Supper

READINGS: Exod 12:1–8, 11–14; Ps 116; 1 Cor 11:23–26; John 13:1–15

REFLECTION: Some of my favorite memories are of special meals eaten with family and friends. Meals, properly done and not simply perfunctory, provide a context for more than simply eating and drinking. They are occasions of true fellowship, conviviality, and sharing. One of the most solid traditions concerning Jesus of Nazareth is the church's memory that on the night before he suffered and died, he dined with his most intimate companions. St. Paul is the one who gives us the vocabulary of "the Lord's Supper" (1 Cor 11:20). In fact, his account of this event, which is recorded in his First Letter to the Corinthians in the context of his having to correct their behavior in that regard, was already "tradition." Paul's version of this important meal is the oldest account of it, antedating the accounts in Mark, Matthew, and Luke by many years. That is why it is chosen as this evening's second reading. Paul begins it solemnly with the words, "For I received from the Lord what I also handed on to you" (1 Cor 11:23). Such vocabulary is recognizable as the way Jews handed on traditions, from one generation to another. Paul goes on to use this memory of Jesus's last meal—perhaps a Passover meal, as reflected in the choice of this evening's Exodus reading—to take the Corinthians to task for not celebrating it in a dignified manner (see 1 Cor 11:17–22 for the context). Jesus most solemnly identified himself with bread and wine, a "new covenant" in his own blood for the life of the world.

The gospel reading chosen for this special Eucharist is also instructive. Surprisingly, John's Gospel is the only one *not* to record the words of institution over the bread and wine. Instead, while Jesus is at table with his chosen ones, he assumes the function of a common servant. He puts on an apron, bends down, and washes the feet of his disciples. These are the actions not of the master but of a lowly house slave. Peter, ever the petulant one, at first refuses to accept this humiliating gesture. After all, Jesus is the Lord and Master. Peter eventually surrenders. Then, after completing the task, Jesus explains: "If I, therefore, the master and teacher, have washed your feet, you ought to wash one another's feet. I have given you a model to follow, so that as I have done for you, you should also do" (John 13:14–15). The combination of these two very different ways to envision the eucharistic action belies its profundity. John's account of Jesus's advice to imitate his humble gesture is made the equivalent of Paul's recollection of Jesus's words, "Do this in remembrance of me" (1 Cor 11:24). Word and deed meet in these two diverse realities. They are really two sides of the same coin. Eucharist is not merely a liturgical ritual that we celebrate Sunday after Sunday. It is also a call to put into action the words that we profess.

St. Augustine sometimes recollected this lesson for his own congregations. When presenting the consecrated bread to the recipients at communion, he sometimes advised them with the words: "Become what you receive." I think Paul's advice to the Corinthians is still pertinent for us today. "Each person should examine themselves, and so eat the bread and drink the cup" (1 Cor 11:28, my translation). Not just this evening, but at every Eucharist, we should ask ourselves if we have put into action what we have celebrated at the table of the Lord.

QUESTION: What does the Eucharist mean to me? How can I improve my capacity to enter into its celebration with whole heart, mind, and soul?

FRIDAY OF THE PASSION OF THE LORD (GOOD FRIDAY)

READINGS: Isa 52:13—53:12; Ps 31; Heb 4:14–16; 5:7–9; John 18:1—19:42

REFLECTION: When I was young, I sometimes thought it odd that we Christians would call this day on which we commemorate our Lord's death "good." Of course, it was then explained to me that the goodness that comes from what happened on this day is nothing less than salvation. That is what makes it good. And it was not merely a miscarriage of justice against an innocent man. It was part of God's salvific plan for wayward humanity. Today, we appropriately meditate on Jesus's passion and death. We are brought before the cross—nay, the crucifix, with its corpus hanging upon it—to reflect on the depth of God's love for sinful humanity.

I am not sure that all Catholics realize there is no *Mass* on Good Friday. In fact, after the celebration of the Lord's Supper on Holy Thursday Evening, there can be no Mass until the Easter Vigil, which is not supposed to begin until Holy Saturday evening. In place of Mass, we have a celebration of the Lord's Passion. Yes, there is a liturgy of the word and the reception of communion, with hosts consecrated the night before at the Mass of the Lord's Supper, but it is not Mass. In addition, there is an opportunity for each attendee individually to reverence the cross, and special prayers are offered for a variety of needs. In short, everything is oriented to strengthen our meditation on the "wood of the cross" which has wrought our salvation.

Appropriately, the first reading today is the fourth and final Suffering Servant Song. It is the most explicit of the four in terms of the intense suffering this innocent individual undergoes. Jesus's suffering under Pilate seemed to directly reference the anonymous Servant in Isaiah: spurned and avoided by people; our infirmities he bore; pierced for our offenses; like a lamb led to slaughter; harshly treated yet silent and not opening his mouth; giving his life as an offering for sin; and so on. When Christians heard this fourth song, there was no other interpretation to offer other than what Jesus endured. The second reading from the Letter to the Hebrews also explains that Jesus "learned obedience from what he suffered" (Heb 4:8).

The version of the passion narrative read this day is always from John's Gospel. It is the most dramatic of the four versions found in the New Testament. Like the other three versions, it has its own emphases, its own portrait. Jesus, for instance, is more in charge and is not simply a victim. He goes to his passion freely. When asked whom his accusers seek, he responds, "I AM (he)," and they fall back because it is the divine name. The interrogation before Pilate is no mere haphazard trial. It is a duel between truth and falsehood, between light and darkness, between a true king and kingdom and a limited, human one. Jesus is also not totally abandoned at the cross, unlike the description in all three Synoptic Gospels. His own (unnamed) mother is present as is the (unnamed) beloved disciple. Before expiring on the cross, Jesus entrusts the one to the care of the other, thus making of them ciphers for the new community of love, the church, that he envisioned. And when the time finally arrives, there is no death cry but a proclamation: "It is finished"—an indication that the very purpose for which he was sent into the world—his "hour"—has now been fulfilled. He can now return to his heavenly Father whence he came.

As with Palm Sunday of the Lord's Passion, the best way to experience Good Friday is to let the readings speak for themselves. Sit with them, reflect on them, enter into them, and you will celebrate well.

QUESTION: Take some moments of reflection before a crucifix this day, and ask yourself: How have I embraced the meaning of the cross in my life? How is it a sign of hope?

ALTERNATIVE MEDITATION: For those so inclined who enjoy classical music, I recommend utilizing some artistic reflections on Good Friday. Listening to a recording of Johann Sebastian Bach's *Passion according to Matthew* (*Matthäuspassion*) or his *Passion according to John* (*Johannespassion*), for instance, can be very moving, especially because of their close use of the Scriptures. Also, Joseph Haydn's *Seven Last Words of Christ,* or one of the famous Requiems (Mozart, Verdi, Duruflé, Berlioz, Saint-Saëns) can be meditative. Even parts of George Frederick Handel's *Messiah* (except for the Hallelujah Chorus more appropriate to the Easter season), can be an aid to your meditations.

HOLY SATURDAY (EASTER VIGIL)

READINGS: Gen 1:1—2:2 or 1:1, 26–31a; Gen 22:1–18 or 22:1–2, 9a, 10–13, 15–18;
Exod 14:15—15:1; Isa 54:5–14; Isa 55:1–11; Bar 3:9–15, 32—4:4; Ezek 36:16–17a, 18–28;
Rom 6:3–11; (A) Matt 28:1–10; (B) Mark 16:1–7; (C) Luke 24:1–12

REFLECTION: The ceremony of the Easter Vigil is the most dramatic and inspiring of the liturgical year. Unfortunately, many Catholics have likely never experienced it firsthand. In the past, it used to begin late on Holy Saturday evening and was a long ceremony. Replete with nine biblical readings and sung responses, along with possible baptisms and confirmations, it could last at least a couple of hours. Those who attend, however, testify to being drawn into its beauty.

The vigil begins in darkness. A new fire is lit from which the new Paschal Candle—the large candle marked with symbolic signs of the crucifix, the Alpha and Omega (Beginning and End), and the calendar year—is processed through a darkened church. Then the one holding the candle chants three times, "Light of Christ" (*Lumen Christi*), to which all respond, "Thanks be to God" (*Deo gratias*). As the procession progresses toward the sanctuary, the congregants' individual candles are lit, and slowly the darkened church is illumined.

Then the Exultet, the ancient proclamation of the resurrection, is sung, while all hold their lit candles. At its end, the Gloria is sung with exuberant melody, and the church is fully illuminated.

The next part of the liturgy is the proclamation of nine readings, most from the Old Testament, culminating in the epistle and the gospel reading. These tell the history of salvation. They are testimony to God's patient outreach to sinful humanity in covenant after covenant, until ultimately the gift of God's own Son achieves what no person could before him—conquer sin and death in the resurrection. A short homily follows that is supposed to help people today understand the ancient roots of this ceremony and its application in our modern lives.

The third part of the liturgy is the ceremony of baptism and confirmation. The catechumens and candidates have been preparing all through Lent for this important step in their lives. On this sacred night, their act of embracing the faith is a sign of hope that Jesus's death was not in vain. He died and rose so that a new family of faith might be born. It is a family not based on blood lines but on discipleship.

In the final part of the liturgy, the Mass continues as usual, leading to the reception of holy communion and a final blessing. At the very end, the deacon or priest adds the word alleluia to the dismissal, "Go in peace" because "alleluia" is *the* Easter word that had been suppressed throughout Lent. Now the alleluia can ring out with full force. It is a celebratory Hebrew word meaning, "Yahweh be praised." We will sing it regularly throughout the fifty days of the Easter season, which concludes with the great solemnity of Pentecost Sunday.

The drama of the Easter Vigil is usually quite memorable for those who first experience it. One hopes, of course, it is well planned and executed, which makes all the difference. But it is such a loaded celebration that it is impossible to dwell on every aspect of it. Suffice it to say that this ancient ritual has been passed through the generations to our own day and that it still proclaims the same message: Christ is risen from the dead, Alleluia, Alleluia! He is truly risen!

Although the gospel reading for the vigil focuses on the discovery of the empty tomb, each liturgical year (A, B, and C) employs, respectively, one of the Synoptic Gospels: Matthew, Mark, or Luke. Two details they have in common are that some of the women who had followed Jesus during his ministry go to the tomb, discover it open, and encounter one or two divine messengers who explain that Jesus is not there but risen. No version describes the actual resurrection, nor is it witnessed by any human. Rather, the resurrection is proclaimed. Ultimately, only faith provides the assurance of the resurrection, which the later resurrection appearances will confirm. Each version also mentions Galilee, thus evoking the place where Jesus's public ministry had begun. Some other details in the narratives vary.

In Year A, Matthew (28:1–10) describes Mary Magdalene and "the other Mary" (28:1) going to "see" the tomb. Matthew also mentions a great earthquake happening while an angel descends from heaven, in keeping with his emphasis on astounding natural phenomena that accompanied the entire earthly existence of Jesus. The angel urges them not to be afraid and to go announce the good news of the resurrection to Jesus's disciples.

Mark's version of the empty tomb story (16:1–7) is used in Year B. He also names certain women but points out that they go to the tomb very early after the sun had risen for the purpose of anointing Jesus's body. They discover the tomb open, the body missing, and a young man in a white robe who announces Jesus's resurrection. Uniquely in Mark, the women are told to announce the good news to "his disciples and Peter" (16:7) that Jesus has gone ahead of them to Galilee. Singling out Peter lends emphasis to his leadership role among the Twelve.

Luke's version of the resurrection and empty tomb story is the one read in in Year C at the vigil. It contains one unique aspect worth noting. Luke names some of the women who went to the tomb on Easter morning with spices to anoint Jesus's body: Mary Magdalene, Joanna, and Mary, the mother of James. They encounter the tomb mysteriously opened and two men in dazzling clothes, who announce that Jesus is not there because he has risen, as he had foretold. The women heed the advice of these two to announce this startling news to the eleven disciples. But when they announce the good news, they are not believed! In that patriarchally dominated society, the testimony of women was not easily accepted. But Peter goes to the tomb anyway and finds it as the women had said. He goes home amazed. An interesting fact to note with regard to this account is that the biblical tradition uniformly accords to Mary Magdalene the honor of being the first disciple to experience the risen Lord Jesus (see Mark 15:40–41, 47; Matt 27:55–56, 61; 28:1; Luke 23:49, 55–56; John 19:25). That is why St. Thomas Aquinas gave her the title, *apostolorum apostola*, the apostle of the apostles.[1] She truly announced the good news to the apostles. She had been one of a group of faithful women who, behind the scenes, had followed Jesus throughout his public ministry and were present at his crucifixion (Luke 23:55). How appropriate that they should bear witness to the risen Lord Jesus on Easter morning.

In sum, the vigil launches the Easter season during which the resurrection appearances and the growth of the church will flesh out important aspects of the Christian faith into which the catechumens and candidates are admitted.

QUESTION: How can I best understand the mystery of the resurrection? How does it serve as a message of hope?

---

1. St. Thomas Aquinas, *In Ioannem Evangelistam Expositio*, c. XX, L. III, 6.

8

SUNDAY OF THE RESURRECTION OF THE LORD: EASTER

READINGS: Acts 10:34a, 37–43; Ps 118; Col 3:1–4 or 1 Cor 5:6b–8; John 20:1–9 or Luke 24:1–12 or, at an afternoon or evening Mass, Luke 24:13–35

REFLECTION: At last, the day of the resurrection is here. Alleluia, alleluia! Our Lenten pilgrimage, which began in ashes, erupts in flames, in the light of the resurrection. Our humble penitential attitude is replaced by exultant joy.

Easter Sunday has several readings to choose from, so to choose just one for reflection is difficult. The biblical readings consist of a mixture of narratives about the postresurrection appearances by Jesus and the challenges these posed to the dejected apostles, and excerpts of speeches testifying to the resurrection. The latter come from the Acts of the Apostles and will feature regularly throughout the entire Easter season. In fact, the forty-day Lenten period is followed by the fifty-day Easter period, leading up the solemnity of Pentecost. It celebrates the gift of the Holy Spirit, Jesus's farewell gift to the entire church.

Rather than a usual reflection on Easter, I propose an alternative. The resurrection is such a mystery that it may be best not to approach it rationally. Rather, a poetic meditation on it may be more useful. One such poem comes to mind. I came across it as a young priest and have come back to it time and again at Easter. It is a good reminder that a great mystery like the resurrection sometimes is best explored through poetry rather than discourse. The poem is by John Shea and is titled "The Resurrection Prayers of Magdalene, Peter, and Two Youths."[1] It reflects on three resurrection appearances: to Mary Magdalene (John 20:11–18), to Simon Peter (John 21:1–14), and to two disciples on the road to Emmaus (Luke 24:13–35). Just sit with the poem and let your imagination take over.

The Resurrection Prayers of Magdalene, Peter, and Two Youths

Like her friend
she would curse the barren tree
and glory in the lilies of the field.
She lived in noons and midnites,
in those mounting moments of high dance
when blood is wisdom and flesh love.

But now
Before the violated cave
on the third day of her tears
she is a black pool of grief
spent upon the earth.

They have taken her dead Jesus,
unoiled and unkissed,
to where the desert flies and worms
more quickly work.

---

1. John Shea, *The Hour of the Unexpected* (Niles, IL: ACTA Publications, 1977), 48–49. Used with permission.

She suffers wounds that will not heal
and enters into the pain of God
where lives the gardener
who once exalted in her perfume,
knew the extravagance of her hair,
and now asks whom she seeks.

In Peter's dreams
the cock still crowed.
He returned to Galilee
to throw nets into the sea
and watch them sink
like memories into darkness.
He did not curse the sun
that rolled down his back
or the wind that drove
the fish beyond his nets.
He only waited for the morning
when the shore mist would lift
and from his boat he would see him.

Then after naked and impetuous swim
with the sea running from his eyes
he would find a cook
   with holes in his hands
   and stooped over dawn coals
who would offer him the Kingdom of God
for breakfast.

On the road that escapes Jerusalem
and winds along the ridge to Emmaus
two disillusioned youths
dragged home their crucified dream.
They had smelled messiah in the air
and rose to that scarred and ancient hope
only to mourn what might have been.
And now a sudden stranger falls upon their loss

with excited words about mustard seeds
and surprises hidden at the heart of death
and that evil must be kissed on the lips
and that every scream is redeemed for it echoes
in the ear of God and do you not understand
what died upon the cross was fear.
They protested their right to despair but he said,
"My Father's laughter fills the silence of the tomb."
Because they did not understand they offered him food.
And in the breaking of the bread
they knew the imposter for who he was—
the arsonist of the heart.

After the end
comes the conspiracy
of gardeners, cooks, and strangers.